Dead-Lock

A thriller

Hugh Janes

Samuel French – London
New York – Toronto – Hollywood

DEAD-LOCK

First presented by Bill Kenwright in association with the Churchill Theatre, Bromley on 9th May 1991 with the following cast;

Diana Chapman	Moira Lister
Victor Fleming	Jack Hedley
Alec Chapman	John Hudson
Paul Chapman	David Pullan
Dr Karen Blackwell	Sarah Jane McKechnie

Directed by **Alison Sutcliffe**
Designed by **Tim Goodchild**
Lighting by **Leonard Tucker**

The action takes place in the main room of the Chapmans' old house

ACT I
Scene 1   A morning in late October.
Scene 2   Dusk two days later.
Scene 3   Early evening the following day.

ACT II
Scene 1   A few moments later.
Scene 2   3.00am the following morning.

Time – the present

COPYRIGHT INFORMATION

(See also page ii)

Author's Notes

The Stairlift
Dead-Lock can be performed successfully using an electric/battery powered wheelchair instead of the stairlift.

Unless it is possible to operate the wheelchair by remote control the changes in action/dialogue are as follows;

Page 2 Additional dialogue only;
   Diana It looks like one. (*She sits*) And don't I have to plug it in — when not in use.
   Alec How did you know how to use it?
   Diana Alec, it has a stop go lever, it isn't Concorde.
Page 7 **Paul** It brings the proms into the home beautifully. (*He switches on the hi-fi*) And illuminates them. (*He switches on a lamp*)
Page 7 **Alec** Give it to me. (*He grabs the remote; Silences the hi-fi and switches off the lamp*)
Page 10 *Finding nothing unusual she turns thoughtfully away when the lamp Paul activated comes on. She moves towards it when the hi-fi booms on with the Bach concerto. Diana stares bewildered — as the* CURTAIN *falls*
Page 15 No change
Page 15 *Dr Blackwell walks upstairs and sits in the wheelchair. She presses the lever and takes it smoothly to the top of the stairs*
Page 19 No change
Page 22 No change
Page 25 No change
Page 36 No change
Page 36 *Victor shines his lamp on the wheelchair and quietly walks upstairs. He carefully turns the chair and wheels it down the ramp to the bottom. He takes a length of cable from his pocket and plugs one end into the wheelchair. Taking out a screwdriver he fiddles with the hand controls and with the area where he has plugged the cable. Satisfied he plugs the other end of the cable into a wall socket and switches on the power. His action continues as script* — Anglepoise — lamp — bulb change – bulb to bin — Paul enters
Page 41 Dialogue change;
   Paul My mother! Helpless in this house because of your little toy. etc;
Page 50 No change.

The Set
The full staircase and gallery can be replaced by a shallow half-staircase of about 7 or 8 steps leading to a bannistered half-landing that goes off R. A wheelchair would run on a ramp fixed to the stairs.

If Paul is unable to be completely hidden in the wing chair before his first entrance on page 3 he should step out quickly from the kitchen instead.

In this version I have described the original set which I considered visually ideal for the style of production. But any large, old, well lived in house could be suitable.

The Location

The location of the house for this first production was somewhere in Surrey about 20 miles from London. However, as long as the distance of house from city is about the same, the location can be anywhere in the world.

Characters' Ages

The playing age of Diana Chapman governs the rest of the casting. This character can be anything from her mid forties to her sixties. Victor is a few years older; Alec about twenty years younger and Paul a few years younger than this. Dr Blackwell should never be less than twenty-five.

Foreign Productions

Colloquialisms like "pub" or "boot" etc may be changed to appropriate references.

For productions in Canada, "Canada" is changed to "Scotland" "Canadian" to "Scottish" and "Moose Jaw" to "Dunoon".

This play is dedicated to Olga and the memory of E.H.J.

ACT I

SCENE 1

The main room of the Chapman's large, old house. It is a sunny, late October morning

The room is attractively decorated and furnished. Much of the woodwork and brick/stone walls have been revealed. The wall, L, is mainly wood shelving, containing an inset door to the old study. DS is an underside section of the staircase that leads into the study. UL is a lobby and heavy front door. UR are garden doors leading to a patio with a garden beyond. Against the wall, R, is a staircase leading to a gallery with a window and exits L and R. Beneath the stairs is an entrance to the kitchen

The shelves are packed with books, photograph frames, objets d'art and a hi-fi. UC is a large desk and chair. On the desk is a computer keyboard and large VDU (both practical), paper knife, telephone with amplifier and an anglepoise lamp. Beside the desk is a waste-bin. Behind the desk, L, is a drinks cupboard. Hanging prominently above it is a large portrait of a strong, moustached man in a fedora; it is Richard. The fedora hangs in the lobby. A large armchair is DS of the study door and beside it is a small table with a vase of flowers. There are two other small tables; one at the foot of the stairs and one near the garden doors which has a lamp on it. There are full-length curtains at the garden doors and upper window. A chiming clock and good pictures are on the walls. A wing chair is partially hidden under the stairs. An electric stairlift runs the full-length of the stairs (NB: see notes for production without a stairlift)

When the CURTAIN rises Paul is sitting in the wing chair, hidden from view. (If this is not possible he should enter from the kitchen) The front door is open. Dr Blackwell enters. She is an ambitious young woman, smartly dressed and carrying Diana's coat and briefcase. Alec follows, carrying Diana's suitcase. He is her elder son, serious and seems older than his years. He wears an ordinary business suit

Alec That's everything out of the car. (*He puts the case down*) Where's mother?

Dr Blackwell In the conservatory I think.

Alec takes the coat to hang in the lobby

Are you sure you can manage her on your own?

Alec Of course.

Dr Blackwell A car crash of that magnitude leaves more than just physical scars.

Alec (*glancing at his father's portrait*) Yes.

Dr Blackwell (*pausing*) I better get back to the hospital; I'm still on duty. (*She starts to go*) Watch her closely for any odd behavioural patterns.
Alec I'll keep you informed. Have you got the pills?
Dr Blackwell Almost forgot. (*She rattles a plastic bottle she takes from her pocket*) As we arranged.
Alec Thank you.

As he takes the bottle their hands touch briefly before she turns and exits

Alec watches her for a moment then shuts the door

(*Calling towards the kitchen*) Mother? Are you there? (*He pauses*) Mother?
Diana (*off*) I'm up here, Alec.

Diana enters upstairs and looks over the banister. She is a smartly dressed, good-looking and determined woman. She uses an elegant stick – as much for psychological as physical need

Alec How did you get up there?
Diana (*holding up her stick*) I pole-vaulted! (*She moves to the stairlift*) How do you think? I used my electric chair.
Alec Don't call it an electric chair.
Diana It looks like one. (*She sits*) Whatever — my new chairway to heaven.
Alec How did you know how to use it?
Diana Alec, it has two buttons, it isn't Concorde. (*She starts the chair descending*)
Alec Be careful. You can only just manage.
Diana Just will do for now. I'll await the spectacular. It doesn't feel very safe. It will probably eject me halfway down.
Alec It's bound to be safe. It has the British Standards Safety Mark.
Diana Next time I'll remember my crash helmet. Though I've come to realize fate has little regard for caution. (*She arrives at the bottom of the stairs*) There — landed. (*She stands*) Has the doctor gone?
Alec Yes.
Diana Good; then you can wheel out the steel band to welcome me home.
Alec I thought you'd prefer a minimum of fuss today.
Diana Fuss — yes. But after five months restoration work on my body I'd have enjoyed a band.
Alec I'll remember next time. (*He moves away*) Are the re-arrangements to your liking?
Diana It all looks very good.
Alec I've done everything as you suggested.
Diana By yourself?
Alec Victor arranged the computer and all the electronics — I organised the rest. I wanted it to be personal.
Diana Didn't Paul help?
Alec No.
Diana Oh.
Alec What did you expect?

Diana I expect he meant to. I thought the garden looked rather neglected.
Alec It's been well looked after.
Diana It has obviously missed my pale green fingers.
Alec Well, you couldn't have left hospital any sooner.
Diana Or any later; I was on the verge of striking the next nurse who told me when to use the telephone. And you can only eat so many grapes.
Alec I'm sure you were a wonderful patient.
Diana I was a wonderful impatient! I hate hospitals.
Alec You'd be dead without that one.
Diana Hum!
Alec Dr Blackwell still isn't convinced you're safe.
Diana She said I was perfectly safe.
Alec She only said that to bolster your confidence.
Diana Then that part of her treatment was most successful. What beautiful flowers.
Alec Guess who? (*He hands her a card*)
Diana "Wanted home to be less like the office. Love Victor." How kind.
Alec (*not being outdone*) Did you see mine in your bedroom?
Diana Yes, thank you.
Alec You haven't changed you mind about sleeping upstairs?
Diana Definitely not.
Alec (*opening the old study door*) It would be no trouble to fix up a single bed in the study.
Diana Sleep downstairs; in a single bed? I'd feel like a nun in a cell.
Alec It would be so convenient. There's plenty of space without the desk.
Diana Good. I shall use it for storage. Richard only worked in there to be perverse. You can hover on the draught down that back staircase.
Alec (*shutting the door*) As you wish.
Diana Would you take my suitcase up please?
Alec Of course. Do you want me to unpack for you?
Diana No. I must find my own routine.
Alec Won't be a moment.

Alec exits upstairs with the case

Diana takes papers and a diary from her briefcase and puts them on the desk. She familiarizes herself with the room then goes towards the kitchen. A hand holding a bunch of flowers is thrust in front of her

Diana My god!

Paul rises from the hidden wing chair under the stairs. He is her engaging and frivolous younger son. He wears smart, casual clothes

Paul No mother — just me.
Diana You nearly gave me a heart attack.
Paul And I was trying to give you flowers.

He kisses her and she hugs him

Diana (*mildly*) You wicked boy.
Paul Pleased to see me?
Diana Of course I am.
Paul Good. It's lovely to see you too.

Alec enters upstairs

Alec Mother? Are you all right?
Diana Yes, Alec.
Alec I thought I heard you yell.
Diana It's Paul. He startled me.
Paul Hello, old brother.
Alec (*coolly*) What are you up to Paul?
Paul Just being a bad penny.
Diana Don't be silly. Bad penny.
Paul Here. Before they wilt.
Diana (*taking the flowers*) Bless you.
Paul A bit unimaginative it seems.
Diana Not at all.
Paul I picked them from the garden.
Alec How thoughtful.
Diana They would have been wasted otherwise.
Paul I didn't mean to frighten you, Mother.
Diana I know you didn't. You always hid in that alcove when you were little. Built a house for yourself out of boxes. You'd play in there for hours.
Paul I liked being out of the way.
Diana You were never in the way.

Paul blows her a kiss. Alec walks downstairs

Alec I've opened your case and left it on the bed.
Paul What a good old brother you are.
Alec I didn't think you were coming today.
Paul I didn't say either way. I thought I'd leave you to organize the parade and arrive in time to wave my flag at the queen.
Alec Helpful as ever.
Paul We leopards and our awful spots.
Alec Would you like some coffee, Mother?
Diana Please.
Paul I'll take what's going.
Alec Such good manners, as ever.
Paul What a stickler you are for convention.
Diana (*interposing*) Alec, have they re-arranged the kitchen much?
Alec Enough so you can sit to do most things.
Paul When isn't she going to be sitting?
Diana Yes. I'm looking forward to a ceremonial burning of this stick.
Paul The Bonfire of the Vanities.
Alec You've been advised to get used to things slowly.

Diana Dr Blackwell would have me forever lying on my back — if you'll pardon the expression.
Alec Because undue pressure might have an adverse effect.
Diana Now that I'm home I can feel my strength returning every minute. Don't I look well to you?
Paul Absolutely blooming, Mother.
Diana Blooming mother!

They giggle

Paul For a complete cure I would prescribe a course of neat champagne.
Diana Coupled with therapeutic hard work.
Paul You work, I'll pour the champagne.
Diana Alec, glasses!
Alec Don't get carried away.
Diana I want some fun.
Alec I merely suggest restraint.
Paul She's been restrained. If she only has strength for one major activity in a day it should be opening a bottle of champagne.
Diana Two bottles. I'll re-discover the boundaries of human endurance.
Alec Yes — back in hospital.
Paul Why don't you just stop fussing for five minutes and make the coffee. Not too black for me — I couldn't bear it!

Alec looks at him a moment before exiting to the kitchen

Diana looks at Paul

Diana Don't upset him.
Paul Glory monger.
Diana He's worked very hard organizing everything for me. He wants it to be just right.
Paul He should get on with his own life and let others lead theirs. A little more frivolity would do wonders for his career.
Diana We won't go into that. This is a lovely surprise; seeing you. I didn't expect it.
Paul I knew Alec was going to be here and thought you might need cheering up.
Diana Yes — and what else did you come for?
Paul Part of the welcome committee.
Diana My darling, I love you very much but I also know you very well – and I do not confuse the two.
Paul Aren't you pleased we have such an understandable shorthand?
Diana It does save valuable time.
Paul Actually, I'd like some money.
Diana Your father left you plenty of money.
Paul He left most of it in trust.
Diana Your father was a judicious man.
Paul No, we just didn't like each other. The point is, how can I enjoy a lavish lifestyle, as befits the offspring of the country's "greatest

publishing tycoon", if I'm impoverished?

Diana Your flattery will get you nowhere. And you are far from impoverished.

Paul I feel impoverished.

Diana Then show me how you can work and climb the ladder. You'll find the rewards dazzling.

Paul I am working. Like the proverbial.

Diana You're playing at it Paul. There's part of the company ready for you to take over. All you have to do is earn it.

Paul Why can't we just sell everything and retire to a magnificent house overlooking St Tropez?

Diana Because we all still have something to prove.

Paul I only want to prove how well I can live on several millions.

Diana Earn it. Why do you want more money anyway?

Paul I want to move.

Diana From that lovely flat?

Paul I've seen a lovelier one. It's beautiful. Everything's designer label. Even the tap water's Italian.

Diana moves away to find the remote control

You're no fun! I had such high hopes for us. I dreamed we could travel the world together, living luxuriously on father's money.

Diana continues searching

What are you looking for?

Diana There is supposed to be a remote control somewhere.

Paul The thing Victor organized?

Diana Yes.

Paul Isn't it on the desk?

Diana I can't see it.

Paul (*helping to look*) What does it look like?

Diana Like a remote control

Paul   Like this?

He finds the remote control hidden by the computer and hands it to Diana. She studies it

Diana Apparently all I do is aim and fire and my prayers are answered.

Paul Try rubbing it. Perhaps a rich genie will appear and rush to me.

Diana is intent

Paul Mother, it isn't Sanskrit. Just press any old button and see what happens.

Diana Front door? Open — close. Garden doors? Open — close. Curtains – I'll try those.

She points at the curtains, presses a button and they close. She is impressed

Paul The curtains move towards the twenty-first century.

Diana Isn't technology wonderful. (*She presses another button and the curtains open*) Wonderful!

Paul How about some music? Hit the deck!

Diana It does that as well? Yes. (*She points at the hi-fi and presses. A Bach concerto comes on loudly*) I love Bach.

Paul They can probably hear it in Brandenburg.

Diana Do them good. (*She switches off the hi-fi with the remote*) Victor is clever to have thought of all this.

Paul He only rang the electronics company.

Diana Whatever he did it will make life much easier.

Paul Does it pour vodka and tonic?

Diana (*sensing Alec's arrival*) Perhaps it summons someone to do it for you.

Diana and Paul laugh as Alec enters with a tray of coffee which he puts on the desk

Diana It works.

Paul These days robots are almost lifelike. (*He takes the remote*)

Alec Is that the remote control?

Diana Yes.

Alec I didn't have a chance to test it. Is it all right?

Diana Excellent.

Alec Good.

Paul It brings the Proms into the home beautifully. (*He switches on the hi-fi*) And provides a taxi service. (*He starts the stairlift ascending*)

Alec Stop playing. It isn't a toy, Paul.

Alec grabs for the remote but Paul moves away and points at the front door. The bolts shoot across

Paul Ooh, I've shot my bolt!

Alec Give it to me. (*He grabs the remote, silences the hi-fi and stops the stairlift*)

Diana Does it lock up? That was always one of your father's tasks.

Alec It does everything. Bolts the garden doors, the front door, activates the alarm. (*He gives Diana the remote*) The buttons are marked. Be sure not to do them by hand it could affect the mechanism. And remember, it only works in this room. There wasn't much practical use for the rest of the house.

Paul So don't point it at the toaster unless you want to cremate the Hovis.

Alec places a cup near Diana

Alec Black?

Diana Thank you.

Alec Paul?

Paul Too kind.

Alec Help yourself.

Alec moves from the tray with his coffee leaving Paul to get his own

Diana By the way, who did you get to replace Mrs Scoble?
Alec I thought you should stick with a cleaner we know.
Diana Your Mata Hari.
Alec She's promised not to interfere.
Diana Alec, that woman has a tongue that could clip a hedge. Not only that, she's got bottle fatigue.

Paul laughs

I found her drunk in the hearth one day surrounded by the pieces of grandfather's Chinese vase. She said a bird flew out of the chimney and knocked her over.
Paul An ostrich stampede wouldn't knock her over.
Alec This is a big house; you must have a help.
Diana Of course — someone. . .
Paul . . .but mother doesn't want Mrs Scoble.
Alec Fine. You organize something.
Paul But you're so good.
Alec I'll look into it. While I'm about it why don't you let me arrange a nurse?
Diana Good God no! I've seen more sensible shoes than Dartmoor.
Alec Then why not leave Victor and I running the company for the time being?
Diana We've been into all that.
Alec It's one thing writing your weekly columns but how will you possibly manage all the things father did?
Diana By clever delegation and being one step ahead.
Alec You can't make executive decisions from here.
Diana Howard Hughes ran an empire from the Nevada desert, with just a telephone and a large box of kleenex.
Alec And look what happened to him. Besides, when father made his will he had no idea. . .
Diana No idea of what?
Alec Of. . .what was going to happen.
Diana No, go on! Say it! After all it's only words and words are our business.
Alec Best put away.
Diana Say it! That I am responsible for killing your father yet have the temerity to go on living.
Alec No-one blames you for what happened.
Paul Then why mention it?

Alec and Paul glare at each other

Diana My body may have been broken but my mind is intact. Richard left me control because he believed I could do it. I shan't abuse his trust with failure.
Alec No, of course. . .
Diana Now I'm out of hospital I intend to run the company. You may not like it but you must get used to it.
Alec I'm thinking only of the practicality and. . .

Paul Leave it out, old brother for gawd's sake. We neither of us got what we want. You're not managing director and I'm not stinking rich, because we were daddy's naughty boys. Didn't do what the great man demanded. Now we're being chastised for the rest of our indeterminate lives. If mother wants to run the "empire" that's up to her. Father was never blinded by love. If he thought she was the right man for the job she probably is. Besides which there's not a damn thing we can do about it. So don't try and stand in her way. (*He kisses Diana*) I won't.

Diana Thank you.

Paul You're welcome. You're also welcome to my share of the responsibility. I don't want that either. Just tell me what to vote for.

Diana Vote for yourself. That's what I want. So did your father, though I admit he had a peculiar way of showing it to you. I want you to make something of your life. Not waste all those talents.

Paul I'll try, my love.

Diana That goes for you too, Alec.

Alec (*pausing*)Yes, Mother.

Paul Not so easy to take is it, old brother?

Alec (*looking at his watch*) I've a meeting at one. (*He gulps his coffee*) I'll see you later.

Diana Thank you for all you've arranged. I'm very very grateful.

Alec (*pausing*) Yes.

They kiss distantly

Diana Bye bye.

Paul Are you going townwards?

Alec I am.

Paul Excellent stuff.

Diana Must you go yet?

Paul If I can scrounge a lift from my old brother.

Alec Will you stop calling me that.

Paul Calling you what?

Alec Old brother.

Paul Why's that, old brother?

Alec I find it irritating.

Paul Perhaps that's why I do it.

Alec Then why don't you grow up?

Paul Because there's a danger I might end up like you.

Alec Then you won't appreciate my company back to town.

Alec goes to the front door

Paul Don't be mean, old brother. We should heed mother's words and discuss our futures.

Alec tries the door. It is bolted. He glares at Paul, starts to pull the bolts by hand, stops and gets the remote

Alec How did you get here anyway?

Paul Taxi.

Alec A taxi must have cost a fortune?

Paul No — only money.
Diana Where's your own car?
Paul Having the oak tree removed from the bonnet.
Alec Is nothing safe in your hands?
Paul Yes, I am. I'm dedicated to it.

Paul and Diana hug warmly as Alec shoots the bolts and opens the door

Paul Bye, Mother. Talk to you later.
Diana Goodbye, Paul. Thank you for coming down. It was sweet of you.
Paul Nonsense. Wanted to see you safely installed. Can't trust Alec — to do everything.
Alec Bye, Mother.
Diana Drive safely.

Paul blows kisses and Alec half-waves as they exit

Diana waves and shuts the door as the car drives away. She sees Richard's fedora, takes it from the hook and looks up at his portrait. She half puts the hat on, decides against it and replaces it. She prepares to start her "changed" life. She finishes her coffee, puts the cup on the tray and picks it up. As she does the curtains start closing and she bangs the tray back on the desk with surprise. When the curtains are closed she carefully goes to examine them. Finding nothing unusual she turns thoughtfully away when the hi-fi booms on with the Bach concerto. Diana jumps and as she moves to turn it off, it stops. In the brief silence that follows the stairlift starts descending. Diana turns with a little cry to watch the seat moving mournfully down, as ——

—— the CURTAIN *falls*

SCENE 2

Dusk. Two days later

Lamps are lit, curtains open, stairlift down, flowers moved, photographs on the shelf turned inwards. The wind blows gently outside

Diana is on the phone, talking sternly and looking at a book list on the VDU

Diana (*on the phone*) I have the list here. A book this brilliant shouldn't drop six places after only two weeks . . . What have you been doing in that office? I'm alarmed at the problems I've uncovered in the last two days. . . Yes, we will . . . Well I don't want you to worry about me. I'm perfectly all right. Goodbye, Alec.

She hangs up, taps a command into the keyboard, looks at the VDU then sighs and rubs her eyes at if she's had enough. The clock begins chiming five, she looks, the phone rings. Before she can answer, it stops. The wind rattles the garden doors. She looks, then goes to try the doors — they seem safe

Look at all the leaves. I must get Mr Marston to clear them up. (*She glances at the portrait*) I always disliked autumn didn't I, Richard?

The phone rings. Diana answers suspiciously

(*On the phone*) Double seven-three-five-two . . . Victor, how nice to hear your voice . . . Well I am charming. . .(*She laughs*) Now flattery could get you a long way . . . Hold on a second while I switch to your technology.

She presses a button for amplified speech, replaces the receiver and continues as she picks up a glass of vodka and tonic

Sorry, what were you about to say?

Victor's voice Only that I rang dead on time and you were engaged.

Diana I have a mystery caller.

Victor's voice If you're accepting other calls during our five o'clock liason I will be extremely jealous.

Diana As if I would. No, the phone just rang then stopped. It's happened a couple of times.

A car is heard in the drive

Victor's voice Sounds highly suspicious.

Diana (*looking out*) Victor! You old fraud!

Victor's voice Guilty. Goodbye. (*He hangs up*)

Diana switches off the phone and unlocks the front door with the remote control

Victor enters. He is an urbane man of about Diana's age. His arms are piled with newspapers, new books and manuscripts and a large bunch of flowers. He backs into the door to close it

Victor I thought I'd phone from the car then surprise you.

Diana A lovely surprise.

They kiss affectionately across his loaded arms

Victor I had a message you wanted these.

Diana I didn't mean for you to bring them.

Victor A perfect excuse to visit.

Diana You don't need excuses.

Victor (*putting the things down*) Only a fleeting visit I'm afraid. I have to go to Frankfurt. (*He offers the flowers*) Here; in case the others are wilting.

Diana Oh . . . you shouldn't. You've already brought me half of Holland.

Victor I'll bring the other half next week. You're looking much better today. Walking stronger too.

Diana I'm exercising regularly.

Victor Splendid.

Diana To and from the drinks cupboard.

Victor It's working wonders. You're a gazelle in motion.
Diana Good old Victor; I can always rely on you for encouragement.
Victor I like the good; you can leave out the old if you don't mind.
Diana A term of endearment.
Victor Why must they always have a sting in the tail?
Diana So they don't pass unnoticed. Now, can I get you a drink? Or some tea?
Victor No, thank you. I'll wait. My flight leaves in two hours.
Diana Fine. (*She looks at the pile of books etc.*) Are these the new manuscripts?
Victor Yes and some regional newspapers and review copies.
Diana (*picking up one book*) I glanced through the proof of this in hospital. I can't remember if I really enjoyed it or if the drugs made it seem wonderful. I shall try and do it justice. Would you find space on a shelf for them please?

Victor takes the books and finds room on a shelf. He is curious to notice the photograph frames turned inwards. Diana opens a newspaper

Diana What has happened to the *Sheffield Gazette*?
Victor You said appoint an editor with a bit of fire.
Diana I didn't envisage a scorched earth policy.
Victor He's concerned about local politics.
Diana Remind him that Communism is history and tell him to put back the gardening. (*She slaps down the paper and turns to the computer*) Have you seen the New York best seller list?
Victor I knew you'd be disappointed.
Diana Disappointed? I'm furious. An early setback like this reflects directly on my judgement.
Victor Oh . . . no. Just one of those things.
Diana *Night Travellers* topped the British list for ten weeks and should be the U.S. number one. There's not much of a ring to the "number nine bestseller".
Victor Strictly speaking books are Alec's department.
Diana I rely on your experience to anticipate anything that could go wrong.
Victor I try not to interfere. You know what he's like.
Diana He said there was an advertising setback.
Victor No — surely. I'll call Bud Mather.
Diana No, I will. This has cost us prestige, I don't want it costing us film rights.
Victor I think I can handle it.
Diana I don't mean to be harsh, Victor, but I must make sure I'm on top of any problems.
Victor Of course you must. You've inherited a small empire not a news-stand on the corner. It's a big responsibility.
Diana I'm starting to realize.
Victor (*warmly*) Don't worry, we empire builders work together on strong foundations.

She relaxes and goes to him for a hug

Diana I wish Alec was as supportive.

Victor So do I. It would help if he didn't swim constantly against the stream.

Diana Probably his way of escaping from Richard's shadow.

Victor Be careful. Alec is a very ambitious man who's ambition has been obstructed. That's a dangerous combination.

Diana (*breaking away*) Don't be so melodramatic.

Victor I'm not. Some men's ruthlessness can be well concealed.

Diana Allow me to know my own son.

The wind shakes the garden doors quite strongly and Diana looks a little wary

Victor Is anything wrong?

Diana The doors shuddering like that took me by surprise, that's all.

Victor What is it really?

Diana Oh . . . just me being edgy living alone for the first time. The house seems bigger — emptier. Sometimes it creaks like a weary ship at sea.

Victor You can't tell me you're that concerned about a few creaks.

Diana No. One or two odd things have occurred.

Victor Oh?

Diana You know how I've always got up at about three in the morning to work.

He knows

Well last night I got up as usual, came to the top of the stairs and could hear something moving down here. I couldn't see anything but I could feel cold air. When I came down I found the front door wide open and leaves blowing round in the lobby. Just leaves — swirling in the wind.

Victor How strange. Are you sure you locked up properly?

Diana I always have done. I check. Alec was most concerned I knew how to do that.

Victor Shouldn't the alarm have gone off?

Diana Yes — and it worked perfectly today when I tested it.

Victor Have you checked the remote control?

Diana Yes.

Victor And you're sure you're. . .

Diana Yes I am pressing the right buttons.

Victor Sorry.

Diana No — I wouldn't be in the least surprised if I had one drink too many and simply didn't fasten the bolts.

Victor Consider yourself lucky no-one took advantage and walked off with the family silver.

Diana Mrs Scoble has probably already done that. Another odd occurrence is . . . (*She points to the shelves*) Those pictures were like that when I came down this morning.

Victor I noticed them when I put away the books but didn't like to say anything.

Diana Faces turned away like that — made me uneasy. I didn't want to touch them.

Victor (*turning them round*) Do you think the door and the photographs are connected?

Diana I don't know what to think. It's all so odd. I wonder if I did it myself – unconsciously.

Victor I wonder if you should cut out drinking one night.

Diana (*laughing*) I'm only drinking by the nip not the bottle — that's only to be rid of my autumn blues.

Victor If you feel that badly why don't we just take off to a smart hotel in the sun and forget about it.

Diana Exactly what Paul wants me to do. Take the money and run.

Victor Maybe he's right.

Diana Not yet he isn't.

Victor Why don't we at least take off somewhere for dinner?

Diana I couldn't possibly dine with you until I know you better.

They laugh

Victor My goodness, how long have we been friends?

Diana I dread to think. You were my first real sweetheart.

Victor You were mine — until I introduced you to my best friend.

Diana (*embarrassed*) Am I forgiven yet?

Victor After all we've been through together. . .? (*He puts his arm round her shoulders*)

Diana I'm glad you didn't leave.

Victor So am I.

Diana Well. . .(*She breaks*). . .I know you well enough to know that as I'm not going to have dinner with you, you want to be on that plane.

Victor Am I that obvious? Oh dear. Shall I drop in and see you tomorrow on my way back from the airport?

Diana Would you?

Victor Be about nine. Anything you need before I go?

Diana Nothing another vodka won't give me.

Victor I can't compete against eighty per cent proof.

Diana You wouldn't settle for less than a hundred per cent.

Victor Didn't get it though did I? Goodnight, Diana.

Diana Goodnight, Victor.

They kiss, Victor opens the front door and exits

Diana goes to the phone, presses an automatic dial button and lifts the receiver

Diana (*on the phone*) Hello Jenny — send a fax please to Bud Mather in New York — to read; Let me have immediate facts regarding *Night Travellers* sudden fall. It is two years since we were at the top, consider a number one book your number one priority. Signed etcetera. I want that on his desk "when" he gets back from lunch. Thank you, Jenny.

She replaces the receiver. The wind rattles the garden doors. She flicks on a patio light and looks out at the black night. The phone rings. She switches off the light. The phone stops, but she lifts the receiver and cautiously listens, hears only the dialing tone and hangs up. She dismisses the phone and takes the flowers towards the kitchen. A door bangs upstairs. She looks up

Who's up there?

She puts the flowers down, gets onto the stairlift and starts it moving up. Halfway up it stops

Damn it!

Diana fumbles with the buttons but the stairlift won't move. She looks up and down deciding which way to go. Suddenly there is a loud knock at the front door. Diana struggles onto the stairs and with difficulty begins to work herself down when the door bursts open with a crash and wind swirls leaves into the lobby. (Optional)

A figure stands in the dim light outside

Who's there?

Dr Blackwell steps into the lobby carrying a slim black file case

Dr Blackwell Is anyone about?
Diana Dr Blackwell?
Dr Blackwell Mrs Chapman! What on earth are you doing?
Diana Having a little difficulty.

Dr Blackwell shuts the door and goes quickly to help Diana down the stairs and into a chair

Dr Blackwell Now be careful. Sit down here. It is imperative that you always use the stairlift. I can't imagine what you were thinking trying to climb the stairs?
Diana I wasn't. The chairlift jammed.
Dr Blackwell Surely not.
Diana Look for yourself.

Dr Blackwell picks up the remote control and presses a button. The stairlift rises smoothly to the top of the stairs. Dr Blackwell looks at Diana

Diana It stopped. Just stopped. I tried the buttons — nothing worked.
Dr Blackwell Well, it seems to be working now; that's the main thing. So you won't have to use the stairs again. That kind of activity is far too much at this stage of your recuperation. I have stressed that.
Diana I was stuck — then the door flew open. I didn't know what was happening.
Dr Blackwell I wondered for a moment if you'd opened the door in anticipation but I see I'm a little early.
Diana Early?

Dr Blackwell For our appointment.

Diana looks

Dr Blackwell You insisted this was a good time of day for you.
Diana An appointment? I'm sorry — I don't remember.
Dr Blackwell That's quite all right. I'm not one of those psychiatrists who has a complex about being forgotten.
Diana Oh no. . .
Dr Blackwell It really doesn't matter.
Diana Please look in my diary — on the desk. What does it say?
Dr Blackwell (*looking in the diary*) There's nothing down.
Diana That's most unlike me.
Dr Blackwell You have our next appointment I see but no engagements today. Five o'clock; Victor; phone call.
Diana You know Victor.
Dr Blackwell Your late husband's partner? (*She gets her filofax*)
Diana Almost — and a very old friend.
Dr Blackwell We haven't actually met; your son told me about him. He's a great help to you, I understand.
Diana I couldn't manage without him.
Dr Blackwell Strong support is vital now.
Diana Yes — could you pass me my drink?
Dr Blackwell Mrs Chapman. . .
Diana You said it was all right.
Dr Blackwell In moderation. (*She hands her the drink*)
Diana Would you?
Dr Blackwell Not for the moment, thank you. (*She looks at her filofax*) Yes, we definitely have an appointment.
Diana I can only apologise for my poor memory.

Dr Blackwell puts away the filofax and takes out a file on which she makes occasional notes

Dr Blackwell You mustn't expect to be quite yourself just yet. How are you feeling physically? Any better?
Diana Much.
Dr Blackwell Following the exercise pattern we outlined?
Diana Yes, following doctor's orders.
Dr Blackwell You look a little tired. Have you been sleeping?
Diana Do you want the truth — or the press release? The truth is I'm half afraid to sleep. I still have terrible nightmares about the crash — and what I did.
Dr Blackwell You did nothing. You've seen the police report. It was an accident. The car crashed through brake failure. You are not to blame in any way.
Diana But I'm still expecting something to happen.
Dr Blackwell That's only natural. Things may take a while to settle down. Although you are in familiar surroundings the conditions are unfamiliar. That, coupled with the highly emotional condition you're still in, can

easily stimulate your imagination.

Diana The front door opening — the chairlift stopping — curtains drawing — are not my imagination. And — the telephone rings.

Dr Blackwell Isn't that what it's supposed to do?

Diana I mean it rings a couple of times and stops.

Dr Blackwell I see. Well, if these things are happening ——

Diana They are. . .

Dr Blackwell —Happening unaided.

Diana I have nothing to do with them. . .

Dr Blackwell But they don't happen by themselves.

Diana Exactly! And do you know what I think? I think it's Richard. Richard — here — in this house.

Dr Blackwell Now Mrs Chapman, I thought in the hospital, we got over all of that nonsense of you husband still being alive.

Diana I was over it till I came back here. Then it all started. The noises. The whispers. I feel sure he's here.

Dr Blackwell You're a rational and sane woman —

Diana You see he was still alive. . .

Dr Blackwell – you must dismiss this idea immediately.

Diana I can see him as he came out from the party — a little drunk — laughing at falling down the last step — then in the car — as I drove through that town; what is it now? — laughing, enjoying himself — right up to the time I lost control — the wheel spinning from my hand — the jolt of the first impact — the tearing of metal — his voice yelling — then the look on his face — that look that keeps haunting me!

Dr Blackwell You must forget these thoughts. Your husband is dead.

Diana But I never saw him after the crash. He could still be alive couldn't he?

Dr Blackwell No.

Diana But I didn't see the body.

Dr Blackwell You were still in intensive care.

As she talks Dr Blackwell goes quickly to the drinks cupboard, pours a glass of water and takes out some pills

Now I want you to sit down and take one of these. It's just a sedative. Here.

Diana is almost forced to take the pill

That's right. Good. Now, we've been through all this. What sometimes happens when people haven't seen the actual body of a loved one, or attended the funeral, they find it hard to accept the death. The loss of someone so close becomes irrational. But you have to accept the word of your relatives and your doctors. Your husband was killed — and was cremated.

The telephone rings. They both turn to it. After two rings it stops

Diana There. There, I told you. It's doing it all the time now.

Dr Blackwell Have you rung the engineers? It could be a fault.

Diana Someone's doing it? Someone's trying to frighten me.
Dr Blackwell Now Mrs Chapman, why on earth would anyone want to
do that?
Diana Richard would. He's playing games with me.
Dr Blackwell Now please. . .

The phone rings again

Diana No. No. Go away. Leave me alone.
Dr Blackwell Please Mrs Chapman.

The phone continues

Dr Blackwell Would you like me to answer it?
Diana It's going to stop. Any moment it's going to stop.
Dr Blackwell It will if we let it ring long enough. (*She answers the phone*)
Hullo. . .Fine.

*She becomes warm and secretive. Diana closes her eyes and rests
her head*

. . . I can't now. She became a bit over-excited but I've calmed her
down. . .Yes, lovely. See you there. Bye bye.

*She hangs up and collects her things. She looks at Diana, whose eyes
are still closed, then glances around the room in a knowing, almost
anticipatory way before exiting*

*The front door stirs Diana. She looks about then lifts a glass and drinks; It is
water. She picks up the vodka; better! Diana considers her circumstances as
she looks slowly around the room and eventually to the portrait of Richard.
She picks up the water, walks to the portrait and throws the water into
Richard's face*

CURTAIN

SCENE 3

Early evening the following day

*The portrait is dry, newspapers and glasses are gone; a red-covered
manuscript is on the desk and two others are on the table. Only the upstairs
lights are on*

*A key is heard in the lock and Alec enters carrying a briefcase and a tray of
food. He shuts the door, puts down the things and switches on the lights. He
notes the two manuscripts then, assuming Diana is upstairs, he examines let-
ters on the desk and picks up the remote. He is about to put it into his briefcase when Diana appears upstairs. Alec hurriedly puts down the remote*

Diana Alec!
Alec Good evening, Mother.
Diana I didn't hear you arrive. Where's your car?
Alec At the end of the drive. I nearly ran over Mrs Scoble bearing down on us with that tray.
Diana She was bringing me some supper.
Alec Why?
Diana I expect it's to eat.

Diana sits on the stair lift and glides smoothly down as they speak

Alec Don't be obtuse, Mother. All the fuss you made about her.
Diana She's on trial. I haven't had much of an appetite. Having food prepared might help.
Alec I've offered to cook, or take you out.
Diana I don't want to bother you or have any fuss. She'll just bring the food in and go. (*She gets off the stairlift and switches off the upstairs lights*) Where's the remote?

Alec shrugs

Diana I left it here on the desk.
Alec What do you want it for?
Diana To draw the curtains.
Alec Oh — here. (*He uses the remote to draw the curtains upstairs then down*) That's cosier.
Diana Is there any reason why the curtains would move by themselves?
Alec (*looking at them*) Slight electrical impulse? A draught? Mice? (*He pauses*) Your imagination.
Diana I had enough of that imagination nonsense yesterday with Dr Blackwell.
Alec She is an expert.
Diana Hum!
Alec How about a drink?
Diana Yes, I need something to relax me in case I imagine tripping over my stick.

Alec puts the remote near his briefcase and pours a vodka and a scotch

Alec You have become rather partial to vodka.
Diana I read the label on the bottle. Drink as much as you wish — falling will be cushioned by euphoria.

Alec gives her the drink

Perhaps that's only on Russian vodka. The true meaning of *glasnost*. Nazdrove!
Alec Would you like ice and lemon? There's none here.
Diana Yes, please.

There is a knock at the front door

Alec You're not expecting anyone are you?
Diana You intercepted my only known visitor.

Alec opens the door and Paul enters

Paul You're lucky to still have a rear end on that executive lump you call a car. Evening, Mother.
Diana Hallo, my darling.

They kiss

Paul Only the brilliance of my driving averted a certain tragedy.
Alec What do you mean?
Paul Bloody stupid parking it across the front of the drive like that. I spun in and nearly took out the boot. I've had to park in the next county.
Alec There was plenty of room to pass if you weren't driving at ninety miles an hour.
Paul Seventy. The drive's a seventy mile limit, didn't you know. Anyway what are you doing parking up there?
Alec I wanted the exercise.
Paul It's brought quite a robust colour to your cheeks.
Alec I'd have moved the car if I'd known you were coming.
Paul What and wreck my reputation as a law unto myself.

As they talk Paul flips through his pocket organiser for a phone number

Alec To what do we owe this unexpected thrill?
Paul I was stood up. Can you believe that, Mother?
Diana Never! Must be the first time since you were about fourteen.
Alec How the mighty are fallen.
Diana Isn't it a bit early in the day for you?
Paul Not if you're taking her to Amsterdam.
Alec God.
Paul I'd planned dinner on a canal boat.
Diana Rather extravagent isn't it?
Paul My motto is start them off with something to remember you by. Like putting your cross in the centre of noughts and crosses — it gives you more options later. Also, if I didn't like her, I wanted to be somewhere interesting as a diversion.
Diana Heartening to hear male chauvinism alive and flourishing.
Paul Nature being what it is, Mother. Have you got old Marston's phone number?
Diana In my diary on the desk. Why?
Paul Hasn't he a little garage?
Diana He used to look after Richard's car there.
Alec What's happened?
Paul About five miles up the road something under the bonnet started rattling like nobody's business. I expect the mechanic who removed the oak tree forgot his chainsaw.
Diana You've had so many problems with that car.

Paul I'll replace it if it'll make you happy.
Alec You can exchange a dented, bottom of the range Porsche for some-
thing terrific secondhand.
Paul Not me, old brother.
Diana You've had your company car allowance for the year.
Paul You suggested I change.
Diana The company finances are in enough confusion as it is. We aren't
forking out for a new car whenever you fancy it.
Paul Why ever not?
Diana Policy, my darling.
Paul That's ridiculous. Come on, Mother. Think of my image. And the
company's. I need a new Porsche.
Alec One of the reporters told me a little joke the other day. A waiter in
a city restaurant calls, "Has anyone got a red Porsche outside, only it's
about to be clamped?" Everyone runs out.
Paul Ha bloody ha. Look at your cloned heap.
Alec Top of the range, for the head of the company.
Diana Not quite.
Alec You know what I mean, Mother.
Diana I think I do. Were you about to get ice and lemon?
Alec Of course.

Alec takes her glass and exits to the kitchen

Paul dials

Diana You do understand about the car?
Paul No, but . . . (*He shrugs*) Are you all right?
Diana Why?
Paul You seem a bit — agitated.
Diana (*pause*) I've been hearing noises in the night.
Paul (*on the phone*) Hullo Mr Marston? Paul Chapman . . . I wonder if you
can do me a favour? I've just come down and there's a terrible knocking
in my car . . . No I can fix it but I need a hydraulic jack and some good
light. . .Terrific. See you then. Bye. (*He hangs up*) He's just finishing his
tea. Take it over in ten minutes.
Diana Good.
Paul What were you saying. . .before?
Diana About the noises last night. And the alarm was switched off again.
I tried to tell Alec — I told him I'd seen the curtains moving but he
just thinks it's my imagination. His constant disbelief is starting to
unnerve me.
Paul I won't have you being upset now, Mother.

Alec enters and Diana indicates silence to Paul

› **Diana** Paul, would you pop upstairs? On my bedside table are some
painkillers. I've a bit of a headache.
Paul For you, Mother. . .the world.

Alec gives Diana her drink, now with ice and lemon

Alec Why don't you take one of your sedatives instead?

Diana If I was any more sedate I'd be comatose.

Alec They're very mild.

Diana How do you know?

Alec Dr Blackwell said they are.

Diana I'm not keen on her. I've always preferred male doctors. I think I'll go back to old Dr Feeny now.

Alec I thought Dr Feeny was a vet.

Diana He examined the horses sometimes as a favour.

Alec The drugs he gave made them high for a week.

Paul (*smiling*) I know.

Alec He is completely ignorant of the term "mild".

Diana Yes, that's true. When cousin Alice collapsed during dinner, Dr Feeny said she had mild food poisoning. She was dead by dessert.

Paul I expect he didn't want to alarm you.

Diana I was alarmed — I thought it was my dessert.

Alec Father's axiom was newspaper owners printed everything and couldn't get alarmed.

Paul Newsroom hound says, "We are not alarmed".

Alec At least I know where the newsrooms are.

Paul Oooh! (*He switches on the upstairs lights as he sits on the stairlift*) How are you getting on with your sedan chair, Mother?

Diana It would be the art of gracious living — if it wasn't essential.

Paul Alec won't have tried it. He's superstitious.

Diana Are you?

Paul (*taunting*) Superstitious.

Alec I wasn't aware trying it was compulsory.

Diana No — of course. . .

Alec It seems wrong that's all.

Diana Wrong?

Alec Yes. Tempting providence.

Paul (*starting the stairlift*) The makers guarantee a broken back isn't contagious.

Alec Don't be so childish.

Paul Su-per-sti-tious. Perhaps you can catch something else — from Dead Man's Pyjamas!

Alec You little. . .

Paul sings extravagantly to foil Alec's anger

Paul   (*singing*) I'll build a stairlift to paradise,
                With a new step every day — dedo dedo dedo. . .
                I'm going to get there at any price,
                If that's the price I have to pay. . .

Paul slides off at the top of the stairs and sings and softshoes along the gallery and exits

After a moment the upstairs light goes off and leaves only spill from the bedroom area. Alec finishes his drink and refills the glass. Pause

Diana What does he mean?

Alec What about?

Diana About superstitions? The pyjamas?

Alec I don't like talking about it.

Diana All right.

Alec You wouldn't like hearing either.

Diana I don't like lots of things I hear.

Alec (*pause*) It started in this house, when we were little boys. Paul would put slow worms in my bed. Or whisper spiders would eat me at night if I made the stairs creak. It got to the stage I didn't know if I was safe to go up to bed. Remember Uncle Philip, who lost his fingers in the war? One hand was a sort of web. Paul told me if anyone touched that hand, their fingers would drop off. Then he'd push me against him.

Diana That was just silly fun; boys' fun.

Alec I didn't consider it fun. I hated it.

Diana He probably didn't realize.

Alec Of course he realized. That's why he did it. He couldn't stand not being the centre of attention.

Diana That's not true.

Alec He loathed it when I read by myself. He had to come and find me and pester me to play with him.

Diana This was such a wonderful place for games. You made hide and seek last for hours. I thought you loved playing together.

Alec I loved playing when father was here.

Diana Because he always sided with you.

Alec No, because he never cheated. I enjoyed playing with you too; except sometimes when the game was over you'd creep off with Paul and encourage him to jump out to frighten me once more.

Diana He was so young then.

Alec Always rush to his defence.

Diana I had to help him so he didn't feel left out. You never said anything was upsetting you.

Alec I expected you to realize. (*He pauses*) Then, when I was sent away to school, there were the initiation ceremonies. Traditional, isn't it. My initiation was Dead Man's Pyjamas. After lights out one night I was forced to take off my own pyjamas and put on a noxious, dirty old pair the seniors had done unspeakable things to. When I had them on, the others held lit torches under their ghostly faces and told me someone had just died in the pyjamas. Died of an appalling contagious disease. My flesh shivers if I remember the feeling of those pyjamas scratching against my skin. (*He pauses, then downs his drink*)

Paul enters silently onto the gallery

Diana I didn't know about all that.

Alec No.

Diana But you shouldn't carry the superstitions of a child through manhood.
Alec Sometimes the unwanted doesn't recognise its place in the scheme of things and hangs around needlessly.

There is a knock at the door. Alec opens it

Dr Blackwell enters. She carries a large manila envelope obscured by her bag

Alec Good evening, Dr Blackwell.
Dr Blackwell Good evening, Mr Chapman.

Alec shuts the door

Hello, Mrs Chapman. It's all right, we haven't an appointment this evening.
Diana Thank goodness. I really would have thought my mind was going.
Dr Blackwell No, Alec is lending me a book.
Alec *Night Travellers* touches on parts of Karen's profession. I thought her opinion would be interesting.
Diana Invaluable.
Alec Where are the spare copies?
Diana I'll get one.

Diana goes to the study door

Dr Blackwell How are you feeling today?
Diana Much more sedate thank you.
Dr Blackwell Good.

Diana switches on the study light from outside and enters

Alec and Dr Blackwell kiss briefly but passionately, then she presses the envelope into his hands and he throws it in his briefcase as. . .

Diana comes out of the study. She shuts the door, switches off the light and hands the book elaborately to Dr Blackwell. Paul has seen everything

Diana With the compliments of Chapman Publishing.
Dr Blackwell Oh, I'd feel happier if I just borrowed it.
Diana Please, keep it and put up with a little misery.
Dr Blackwell Well, thank you. (*To Alec*) I'm afraid I must go.
Alec I'll see you out.
Diana Good-night.
Dr Blackwell Good-night, Mrs Chapman. See you on Friday.
Diana Mmm!

Alec opens the door and as Dr Blackwell exits they touch hands and he whispers in her ear

Alec watches her a moment before shutting the door

Alec (*pausing*) Is your drink all right, Mother?

*As Diana looks for her drink Alec slips the remote into his briefcase –
replacing it with an identical one he takes out. He closes the lid without
locking it*

Diana Delicious.

*Paul, having seen all this, crosses the landing to the stairlift and affects an
"RAF" voice*

Paul Scramble squadron. Scramble. (*He sits*) I say this new Lancaster
stairlift seems hunky-dory Winco. Idiot proof. Not quite that advanced?
Never mind. Chocks away. (*He starts the stairlift with an "engine"
noise*) Lets bring one home for Blighty. (*He hums the "Dam Busters"
theme between speaking*) Coming in over the Merner Dam now. Visibility
perfectly clear apart from thick fog. We're going for it. In my sights now.
Perchom! Pills gone. (*He throws the pill bottle at Alec who fumbles
the catch*)

Alec Damn!

Paul Target breached. (*He gets off the stairlift at the bottom, switches off
the upstairs lights and sidles towards Alec's briefcase*) Hadn't you better
give mother the tablets, old brother. She'll have a head like an anvil
otherwise.

Alec Oh, yes.

*As Alec takes the pills to Diana, Paul lifts the lid of the briefcase, pockets
the remote and closes the lid. Alec turns, but sees nothing*

Paul I'm slipping over to Marston's now.

Diana Will you be back?

Paul See how it goes. (*He kisses her*) Don't wait up.

*Paul goes quickly to the door and surreptitiously whisks away the fedora
as he exits*

*When Paul opens the door the wind can be heard quite strongly outside.
When the door is shut the wind quietens but remains audible until the end
of the scene*

Alec Very abrupt exit for our Paul.

Diana I expect he's worried about his car.

Alec He's never worried about a thing in his life.

Diana You must stop being so bigoted about your brother.

Alec Years of experience have lead me to the truth.

Diana Enough to satisfy you.

Alec If you like. (*He picks up the manuscripts*) How did these get here?

Diana Victor brought them down.

Alec I've been looking all over the office for them.

Diana I wanted to read them. I left a message with Jenny.

Alec I was going to bring them. Victor has no business interfering with my
arrangements.

Diana He was doing it as a favour.

Alec I won't have manuscripts disappearing out of my office without my knowledge. When did he bring them?

Diana Last night, on his way to Frankfurt.

Alec Frankfurt? (*He pauses*) I've dealt with everything in Germany. Why ever would he go there?

Diana He's coming over about nine. Ask him. I trust Victor to know what he's doing and do it properly.

Alec In my view you've given him far too much authority.

Diana He knows the company inside out. And he's my oldest friend.

Alec He takes advantage of that. Don't give him undue credit. Father was about to put my name on his office.

Diana He was not.

Alec He was going to buy him out. He suspected he'd been defrauding the company for years.

Diana He what? Never for a second did Richard indicate . . . I won't even discuss such a wicked fabrication.

Alec No, let's not discuss anything whilst you and Victor have it nicely tied up between you.

Diana What does that mean?

Alec Only I've noticed you're under a great deal of stress. I suspect you're having a breakdown and intend bringing it up at the next board meeting. After all, the shareholders and staff shouldn't suffer because the chief executive has over-committed herself.

Diana How dare you. I am not suffering from any stress.

Alec One of the prime symptoms is the inability to recognise it within oneself.

Diana I can assure you I'm perfectly *compos mentis*.

Alec I have Dr Blackwell's report that corroborates my theory.

Diana Ah, so that's what this is all about? I've known for months about the little affair going on between you. I may have been on my back in the hospital but I wasn't out for the count.

Alec You're on the edge. One small event could tip your balance. All this imagining things. Father. Curtains. Leaving the front door open at night.

Diana How do you know about that?

Alec You told me — the other night.

Diana I haven't mentioned it to you.

Alec Don't tell me you're forgotten that now?

Diana I never said a word to you about the front door.

Alec Then how would I know?

Diana I wonder.

Alec I'm concerned for your safety, Mother, alone in this big house.

Diana You're only concerned for your position in the company.

Alec And you're such a model of family love. It would be nice to still think of this as home not just your annex of the office. Isn't it enough that I work for you?

Diana I don't want you to work for me, I want you to work alongside.

Alec On a lead that doesn't actually humiliate me in front of the staff but stifles any initiative. Then the stale tobacco in the editor's meetings can choke any whiff of nepotism.

Diana Perhaps you hadn't realized that without nepotism a family business stops trading.

Alec I should be head of this business. Father promised his position to me. I intend to take it one way or another.

Diana Who do you think you are? Beaverbrook? Randolph Hearst? It takes more than ambition to play the tycoon. You have to know the difference between a headline and a deadline. Richard tried to show you. In the end I had to become his pupil out of sheer necessity. He encouraged you with every weapon in his armoury but you smart Alec, you thought you knew it all.

Alec We've never found out that I don't.

Diana You couldn't zip your flies if they didn't run in a straight line.

Alec For someone so well-bred Mother, you possess a coarse mouth.

Diana I find it the only effective way to get through to you.

Alec Well you have. I've been thoroughly reprimanded haven't I? Perhaps one day I shall see the error of my ways. Or are you just waiting for Paul to grow out of his protracted adolescence? You might have a long wait.

(*He angrily locks his briefcase and marches with it to the front door*)

Diana Where are you going?

Alec To the pub. Perhaps there I can get some decent conversation with my drink.

He storms out

Diana considers a moment then finishes her drink and plonks the glass down. Using the remote she shoots home the front door bolts, switches the hi-fi on low, and dims the lights so only her desk lamp, the portrait light and the table lamp by the garden doors are left on. She sits, opens the red manuscript and begins typing notes. She works distractedly for a while then suddenly the phone rings stridently. She looks at it uneasily before deciding to answer. She slowly reaches across the desk to press the amplifier

Diana Double seven-three-five-two. (*She pauses*) Hallo?

A strange, man's voice whispers through the amplifier

Man's voice Diana.

Diana Who are you? Who's there?

Man's voice Diana.

Diana Go away! Leave me alone! (*She bangs off the amplifier and looks at the portrait of Richard. She gets up and pours a stiff vodka, grabs the ice bucket and finds it empty*) That boy wouldn't bring me ice in winter.

As she moves towards the kitchen the garden door curtains open very slowly about a foot and stop. Diana freezes. After a moment she carefully puts down the bucket and moves cautiously towards the doors. When she is close she stretches out her hands towards the curtains and the doors burst violently open. The wind soars, the table lamp crashes to the floor and all the lights go out. The music increases

*Almost instantly a low light comes on outside, silhouetting a man in a
fedora standing at the garden doors. Diana screams and falls to the
floor, the light outside goes out and there is a loud knocking at the front
door as —*

the CURTAIN *falls*

ACT II

SCENE 1

A few moments later

As the curtain rises there is a loud knocking at the front door. Diana lies where she fell, terrified. The wind is low. There is a final knock at the door. Diana hauls herself to a sitting position. A bright light shines at the garden doors; a moment later Victor enters carrying a powerful lamp

Diana Who is it?
Victor (*pausing*) Diana! It's me, Victor.

Victor puts the lamp down and goes to her

Diana Oh, thank God it's you.
Victor Whatever's happened? Are you hurt?
Diana No, nothing serious.
Victor Are you sure?
Diana Yes.
Victor Here, let me get you up and into a chair. Easy now. Mind how you go. There.

He helps her to a seat. She is agitated and in discomfort but not pain

Diana I am so relieved to see you. I've never been so frightened in all my life.

Victor switches the lights on and his lamp off

Victor You're perfectly safe now. I'm only glad I arrived when I did. (*He feels her brow*) Your head feels quite cold. I'll get you a blanket?
Diana No, the rest of me is boiling. I'll blend soon.
Victor Just stay where you are then. (*He picks up the phone*)
Diana Who are you phoning?
Victor The hospital. You must see a doctor.
Diana I don't want a doctor. I see too many doctors.
Victor Don't be ridiculous. You've had a nasty fall.
Diana Please put down the phone.
Victor I want to know you're all right.
Diana Please!

Victor hangs up

Victor You can be infuriatingly stubborn at times.
Diana I'm just bruised, not badly hurt. I've fallen off enough horses in my life to know the difference.
Victor You look very shaken up. Can I get you anything?

Diana My drink please. It's just there.
Victor I meant medication.
Diana That is medication. Even my doctor said so.

Victor passes the drink

Diana Help yourself.
Victor No, I'm all right. Do you feel up to telling me what happened?
Diana I'm so confused by it all. I remember sitting at the desk working —
the phone ringing — then the curtains opening by themselves. I went over
to look and the doors suddenly flew open with tremendous force. I must
have twisted away, lost my balance and fell.
Victor You're lucky you weren't seriously hurt.
Diana I think I blacked out for a moment. I don't remember much else.
Victor How did the doors open like that?
Diana I don't know.
Victor Did somebody break in?
Diana I don't think so. It was all so fast, so confusing.
Victor Try to remember.
Diana I tell you I don't know.
Victor I'm sorry. I didn't mean to pressure you. It's a shock finding you
like this.
Diana I wish I could remember clearly.
Victor Don't worry now. Take your time. (*He picks up the fallen table
lamp*) Was this on? (*He pauses*) Diana?
Diana Sorry. I was miles away.
Victor This lamp. Was it switched on when it fell over?
Diana Yes . . . or was it? I expect so, it usually is.
Victor Best not touch it. The bulb has smashed in the socket and might
blow a fuse if you plug it back in. (*He coils the flex and puts down
the lamp*)
Diana Will you bolt the garden doors?
Victor Of course. (*He starts closing them*)
Diana Use the remote. You'll damage the mechanism.
Victor You can close them manually.
Diana Alec told me always to use it.
Victor He knows the remote is just for your convenience. We arranged it
that way.
Diana (*puzzled*) He was so definite.

*Victor closes the doors and appears to lock them. The wind fades and is not
heard again*

Victor There was a terrific gust of wind as I arrived. Enough to blow them
open if they were only pushed to. There, tight as a drum.

He draws the curtains. Diana looks intently

Diana Oh!
Victor What is it?
Diana Seeing you there reminded me. . .The figure.

Victor Figure?

Diana Standing in the doorway. It looked like Richard — it must have been you.

Victor Me?

Diana Yes. Wearing Richard's hat.

Victor I don't know what you're talking about.

Diana Look! It's gone.

Victor What's gone?

Diana Richard's hat.

Victor lifts the fedora from a hook in the lobby

Victor Diana, Richard's hat is here. Where it always hangs.

Diana No — that's not where it hangs. It always hangs on the other side. Victor, I saw you.

Victor You saw me enter through those doors and help you up. I wasn't wearing a hat. (*He replaces it*)

Diana Before that.

Victor What do you mean?

Diana As the doors flew open. There was a light — your torch — and you standing there ——

Victor That wasn't me.

Diana —silhouetted for a moment.

Victor I was banging at the front door the whole time.

Diana Not the whole time.

Victor No . . . When I heard you scream I came round to the patio to see if I could get in.

Diana Well, if it wasn't you — didn't you see anyone?

Victor No.

Diana There was somebody at those doors. You must have seen the light.

Victor That was probably my lamp. It might have shone towards the patio when I was by the front door.

Diana It was so bright.

Victor Perhaps it reflected on the glass as the doors opened. What you saw was a trick of the light.

Diana No. It wasn't my imagination.

Victor Calm down. I didn't say that.

Diana But you don't believe I saw anyone, do you?

Victor It's not that I disbelieve but remember that state you've been in. Your depression. The strange events in the house. With that playing on your mind what you saw might have been the shadow of the curtains. Or a shape they made.

Diana I accept my mood. I also know I was falling and taken by surprise but I definitely did not see curtains. (*She pauses*) It must have been Richard.

Victor What are you saying?

Diana Standing — for a moment — in that doorway.

Victor Diana, Richard is dead.

Diana So everyone keeps telling me. Then who was it? A spectre I'm conjuring up? Perhaps I'm super-natural. Why not instigate a witch hunt? Yes that's it, get out the ducking stool. If my vodka and I bob up three times you can just burn me for a rich imagination.

Victor All right. All right. Let's assume there was a figure. . .

Diana There was.

Victor That's what I'm saying . . . Then it was most likely a prowler or a burglar.

Diana Burglars don't normally break in to occupied rooms in the middle of the evening. It's bad for business.

Victor Supposing he was reconnoitering the house and taken by surprise?

Diana I have a strong feeling — whoever it was — was looking for me.

Victor Aren't you being a little paranoiac?

Diana Being paranoiac doesn't mean you're not being followed.

Victor You only caught a momentary glimpse.

Diana If it was only a shadow it at least suggests — for the first time — I was not imagining all the other incidents.

Victor Then we must assume whoever's doing it has access to the house.

Diana I know.

Victor Well — presumably we can rule out Mrs Scoble?

Diana We may not be bosom buddies but — presumably.

Victor Then there's Paul?

Diana Oh no, not my Paul. Besides he went over to Mr Marston's to do something to his car.

Victor Mr Marston doesn't have access?

Diana Of course not.

Victor Well, that's six possibilities removed.

Diana Six?

Victor A prowler, Mrs Scoble, Mr Marston — Paul — Richard and me.

Diana (*pausing*) Yes.

Victor You do accept now it wasn't me?

Diana Of course I do. But I still can't get Richard out of my mind. (*She looks up to the portrait*)

Victor Now Diana. . .You are just trying to deny the obvious.

Diana Alec?

Victor Yes, Alec.

Diana I hoped we could find another answer.

Victor There isn't one. To start with the obvious, his car is parked very strangely across the drive.

Diana Oh yes, he left it there when he arrived.

Victor Why is it still there?

Diana We had a dreadful argument. He stormed out and went to the pub.

Victor How long ago?

Diana A few minutes before you arrived.

Victor I passed the pub and didn't see him on the road.

Diana He would have used the short cut throught the garden. He left in a muddy shoes sort of mood.

Victor That means he could have engineered those doors.

Diana Yes he could. . .but I can't believe it.

Victor Remember, we're not just talking about this. There's all the other things as well.

She knows

What was your argument about?

Diana What are they ever about — his envy of you and his lack of any real power or position.

Victor It fits you see. His resentment of everything bubbles just beneath the surface.

Diana Tonight there was a strange edge in his voice I haven't heard before.

Victor What sort of edge?

Diana As if he was living very close to his limits.

Victor "And coming events cast their shadows before."

Diana Surely Alec wouldn't do anything — irrevocable?

Victor He nearly did tonight. He could get away with it if he made it look like an accident.

Diana Or if he made me seem unbalanced. I found out tonight his wounds go back a long way.

Victor Oh?

Diana You remember when the boys were small, how we used to play in this house? Trying to scare each other. I thought we all considered it fun — Alec didn't.

Victor Didn't he? He scared me one night. You and Richard had gone out and I was looking after the boys. I was alone in here reading and Alec must have sneaked down the back stairs beside his room and into the old study. He wormed a stick through a crack in the plaster behind those shelves and pushed one of the books flying onto the floor in front of me. God it made me jump. (*He pauses*) What does he gain by all of this?

Diana Richard left him the company in the event of my early death, or incapacity.

Victor Alec?

Diana Yes, Alec. You know how much Richard loved him. And how guilty he felt at being away so often when he was growing up.

Victor What would happen to me?

Diana You would remain as you are.

Victor Under Alec. How considerate.

Diana But what Alec hasn't taken into account is my will. In which you become head of the company before him.

Victor I see. Where would Paul fit in?

Diana I've taken care of him financially. And left him options to develop freely within the company. He'll settle to it in a year or two.

Victor For your safety's sake the best thing is to get Alec out of the way for a while. Give him time to simmer down. Why not bring forward our plans to open a Canadian office. You could send Alec over immediately for exploratory discussions. Make it look like a promotion. A vote of confidence.

Diana He'll hate going to Canada.

Victor At the moment the only thing we must consider is your safety.
Diana Yes. You're right.
Victor Good. I'm glad that's settled. Oh, I forgot, I brought you something from the United Germany. I left it in the car. (*He goes*) I wouldn't mind that drink now.
Diana Scotch?
Victor Perfect.

Victor picks up his lamp, unbolts the front door and exits pulling the door to

Diana goes to the drinks cupboard and as she pours a light snaps off, then another and another so only Richard's portrait is illuminated. Diana waits in tense silence. There is a click and the study door slowly opens — after a moment the upstairs curtain opens a little admitting a glimmer of moonlight and the eery voice from the telephone (Alec), we hear from upstairs

Alec Diana
Diana Go away! Leave me alone!

Victor enters carrying a wrapped gift and shuts the front door loudly as the study door shuts

Victor Whatever are you doing in the dark?

He switches on the lights and puts down the gift

Diana (*strangely*) I'm not giving in to him.
Victor Pardon?
Diana I'll fight him with every fibre in my body.
Victor Who are you talking about?
Diana You know who I'm talking about.
Victor Do I?
Diana Yes. He was there in the shadows. (*She points upstairs*)
Victor I can't see anyone.
Diana He wouldn't appear to you. Richard's come for me.
Victor He's not coming for anyone. Don't you understand? Richard is dead and buried.
Diana You must have noticed this time. All the lights went out. He spoke to me.
Victor We've already been through all this.
Diana He spoke to me from up there.

Victor switches on the upstairs lights

Victor Look — there's no-one there. What you heard were creaks. What you saw were shadows created by the moonlight. Nothing more than shadows. (*He switches the lights off*) You have just had a most terrible shock. It's no wonder things aren't as they seem. (*He pauses*) Alec has driven you to this. (*He pauses*) And I've thought of another reason, apart from power. Did you know he holds you responsible for the break-up of his marriage?
Diana That's totally ridiculous.

Victor When he and I were running things we often had boardroom lunches. One day he had a few glasses of wine too many and started rambling on about Clare. How everyone thought Clare was good for him — but you felt he was becoming too strong with her at his side. So you began making her feel unwanted and inadequate until eventually you managed to drive a wedge between them.

Diana I liked her; we got on well. That's simply not true.

Victor I didn't think it was but I thought you should know how he felt.

Diana The truth is, and no-one else knows this, Clare told me that in four years Alec only consummated their marriage twice.

Victor My God!

Diana You see how inadequate that makes him feel.

Victor So to compensate for that he has to take your place in the company.

Diana He's suggested taking your place. Then he could confront me head on.

Victor I must look to my laurels.

Diana He even tried accusing you of fraud.

Victor What!

Diana Don't worry, he knows the way I feel. It won't change a thing where you are concerned.

Victor Thank you. I shouldn't have to rely on your generosity. I know Richard and I weren't equal partners but after all our years together I expected him to leave my position secure.

Diana That was the kind of man he was. He took everything if no-one bothered to stop him.

Victor Yes. (*He pauses*) You must be exhausted.

Diana I'm not sure what I feel.

Victor At least tonight you will sleep like a log I imagine.

Diana Until I get up to work.

Victor You shouldn't.

Diana Perhaps I should give it all up and buy a bungalow in Bexhill.

Victor Hardly your style.

Diana Bungalows or Bexhill?

Victor Either. It's a penthouse in Park Lane for you.

Diana Thank you for your faith in me.

Victor (*pausing*) Would you like me to stay?

Diana Thank you but I think I'll be all right.

Victor I could remind you of happy times we've spent together. Like that summer in Greece before you were married.

Diana I've forgotten all my Greek.

Victor Thank goodness. The only way to stop you talking was push you under the sea in a mask and snorkel.

Diana That was a perfect holiday.

Victor Yes it was. On the plane back from Frankfurt just now I remembered how happy we were; and thought we could be again. Over thirty years is long enough to wait. Why be reticent? Why not ask her to marry me?

Diana Victor. . .

Victor I've taken you by surprise.

Diana Yes. . .I'm very flattered. . .but were you to ask I suspect I'd say I

value you too much as a friend to risk losing that to a husband.
Victor Ah. How very diplomatic. What a funny way life has of cheating
one.

They go to the front door

Tonight hasn't worked out at all as I anticipated.
Diana For either of us.
Victor Are you sure you don't want me to stay?
Diana I must find out myself whatever's happening here. I'm not giving in
to it until I know what it is.
Victor I hope that won't be too late.
Diana It won't be.
Victor You must rest. Why not take one of your sleeping pills?
Diana All right. To please you.
Victor Good. Well, you know where to find me. Good night, Diana.
Diana Good night.

They kiss and Victor exits

*Diana pushes across the front door bolts, walks back into the room and
looks at the portrait. She picks up the paperknife from the desk as she
walks over and sits on the stairlift. She turns the upstairs lights on and
the downstairs ones off and looks up*

Diana All right, I'm waiting.

*She starts the stairlift and the clock strikes the first of ten. Upstairs, she
cautiously crosses the gallery and exits*

*The lights go off, except from the bedroom area. After a moment this also
goes off and the room is black save for a faint glow from the VDU. Pause*

*A lamp shines in through the garden doors; after a moment they open and
Victor enters, closing the doors behind him*

During Victor's action Paul opens the study door for his entrance

*The door must be silent and there must be absolutely no light spill. The only
light on the stage is the faint VDU glow and Victor's lamp as he works*

*Victor shines his lamp on the stairlift, presses a wall button at the bottom of
the stairs and the stairlift descends. As it does he goes to the desk, switches
the anglepoise lamp quickly on and off, then moves to the lamp by the doors.
He puts on a work-glove and removes the smashed bulb. He removes the
bulb from the anglepoise and appears to push the broken bulb in its place.
He puts the anglepoise back in position, pockets the glove and leaves the
bulb on the desk. He goes to the stairlift, lifts the control arm and using a
screwdriver, fiddles about with the wires. He lowers the arm and tampers
with the control panel on the side. Satisfied, he goes to the front of the desk
then turns to shine the torch on the stairlift for a final check. He remembers
the bulb and picks it up. As he bends to drop it in the waste bin Paul rushes
across the room and thrusts a hand gun against his neck*

Paul Hoist 'em!

Victor (*startled*) Ah!

Paul Well well, if it isn't dear old Uncle Victor.

Victor What are you doing, Paul?

Paul What are you doing creeping about?

Victor Making sure Diana's all right.

Paul You went five minutes ago.

Victor My. . .car won't start.

Paul Do I believe that?

Victor Of course you do. For God's sake put the gun down. You've nearly given me a heart attack as it is.

Paul No I won't. I'm just going to blow you away you filthy intruder. Bang!

Paul thrusts the gun violently and pulls the trigger. Victor recoils in horror. A flame comes out of the gun. Paul laughs, switches on the lights and reads the side of the gun

"Presented to Richard Chapman — Smoker of the Year 1977 — by *The Telegraph* Crime Desk." Somebody liked him.

Victor You little bastard.

Paul Ssh! (*He indicates Diana upstairs*) Temper temper! Mustn't get executive strain? You look quite peeky.

Victor It's all such a bloody game to you isn't it?

Paul If I can make it one — yes. So much better than real life. (*He looks at the doors*) You haven't answered my question. What are you doing here? You were supposed to have locked those doors.

Victor I left them unlocked on purpose. I was worried about your mother. I wanted to stay tonight but she insisted she was all right on her own. I left them unlocked so I could get back in and make sure she was protected.

Paul Considerate but sneaky. What's the matter with the car?

Victor I. . .don't know. Probably the battery. The lights won't work and neither will the car phone.

Paul Well — (*He turns the phone*) — in that case feel free to use the advanced technology.

Victor Thank you. Better ring the RAC. (*He reluctantly picks up the receiver*)

Paul Yes, bring on the cavalry.

Victor What does that mean?

Paul You've been caught on the prowl and want to run.

Victor If it comes to prowling, how did you get in? (*He replaces the receiver*)

Paul Oh I spent a quiet evening hiding in the old study listening to you and mother tete-a-teting.

Victor That's despicable knowing the state she's in.

Paul Yes but I didn't know the state you were in. I wanted to find out. I knew she was safe with me ready to leap to her rescue. However, it turns out you and I are thinking along the same lines.

Victor We are?

Paul A highly unstable character my old brother.
Victor No doubt about it. That's why I want to be here. I'm glad we're together on this, Paul
Paul Rottweiler Incorporated!
Victor We should find out how Alec's playing these tricks.
Paul If you say the magic word I'll show you a trick, Uncle Victor. (*He pauses*) Come on. (*He pauses*) Remember? Play the game.
Victor Iz. . .?
Paul That's the one.
Victor Izzy wi. . .
Paul Now don't be shy.
Victor (*quickly*) Izzy wizzy let's get busy!

Paul holds up two remote controls

Paul Voila! Two remote rabbits from the same hat.
Victor Two? I don't understand?
Paul This one is your original that Alec returned tonight. (*He puts it on the desk*) Mustn't get them confused. This one I took from his briefcase after he switched them and while I was at old Marston's I examined it. It doesn't take an expert to see it's been tampered with. I was intrigued to see how it worked. So I crept back here and saw Alec storming out across the garden. Of course these shouldn't work outside this room. But no sooner had I pressed a button than the bolts flew back, a gust of wind whipped across the patio and whoop — Victor's your uncle, the garden doors burst open as easy as your secretary.

Victor looks

Paul Sorry. Touch a raw nerve did I? Anyway, as they flew open you arrived out of no-where — (*he shines Victors lamp*) — carrying this beacon from the Eddystone lighthouse. I'm amazed mother didn't recognise me standing there; (*He puts on Richard's hat*) but I had borrowed the old man's titfer. My hair and high winds do not get on. I breezed in ready to be heroic but poor mother was out of it. Then you rushed up like the Four Horsemen of the Apocalypse and I nipped in there.
Victor So you were the figure in the doorway.
Paul They seek him here — they seek him there. . .
Victor . . .but Alec's causing trouble everywhere.
Paul (*replacing the hat*) Actually, mother's been causing most of it herself. Inadvertently. Press — and the doors close — and Alec arranged it so that later it reversed the programme — and they open. All on a time delay. Very impressive. Everything mother pressed simply turned against her. No wonder he told her always to use it. She was springing her own surprises.
Victor I underestimated Alec's imagination.
Paul I didn't underestimate it, I never knew he had one.
Victor Diana shouldn't be left alone with him.
Paul That's why I looked for the gun amongst father's armoury. (*He takes*

the gun out and lights it) A family that lights together, fights together. There's also the business of the car.

Victor I'll sort that out tomorrow.

Paul Father's car.

Victor Oh . . . Well that's all cleared up isn't it?

Paul Not for me it isn't. Did you see the wreckage? That grand old car, twisted like wire, left to rust into father's blood. Grim. That was no accident. The police ignored old Marston because he's not a recognised mechanic but he loved that car. We're certain, while mum and dad were at the party, someone tampered with the brakes.

Victor Well . . . If Alec is clever enough to rig up all this he is certainly clever enough to fix some brake fluid.

Paul Brake fluid? Yes. (*He pauses*) He's capable of anything my old brother. Best tackle him together when he gets back from the pub. (*He unbolts the front door by hand*) There, let the storm tossed sailor find his way to the rocks.

Victor The only thing is, Diana didn't want me to stay; she mustn't know I'm here.

Paul She won't until we nail him.

Alec and Dr Blackwell are heard off

Damn it! There's someone with him. In here.

Victor and Paul nip into the study

A key is heard in the front door then Alec enters with Dr Blackwell and puts down his briefcase

Alec Don't worry. She's always in bed by this time. And with those pills you gave her she'll be out like a light.

Dr Blackwell Your mother is so territorial. I feel as if I'm committing a crime coming in without her knowledge. That's what living with three men does to you.

Alec I didn't know you'd been living with three men.

Dr Blackwell (*as if asking again*) Please let me see my report.

Alec I keep telling you, your report is perfect.

Dr Blackwell I want to check it. (*She pauses*) Please. To relieve my troubled mind.

Alec All right. For that lovely mind. (*He opens his briefcase and sees the remote is gone*)

Dr Blackwell Something the matter?

Alec Er. . .yes. I've just misplaced something important that's all. Not to worry.

He hands Dr Blackwell the envelope and she takes out the report

It's as we agreed. You've written nothing that isn't true.

Dr Blackwell (*reading*) No, I suppose not. Your mother is in a highly emotional state. And prone to imaginative outbursts.

Alec The board will realize she is still under stress and agree I take some of

the burden of her responsibility. It's for her long term good.
Dr Blackwell Yes, Doctor!
Alec We're getting nearer our goal. You've been brilliant with her.
Dr Blackwell I hope it's worthwhile.
Alec (*returning the envelope to his briefcase*) It will be. Nightcap?
Dr Blackwell Haven't you had enough?
Alec Who knows how long tonight might be?
Dr Blackwell (*coming close to him*) I can't stay.
Alec A little.
Dr Blackwell If we're seen any more together people will know it's collusion.
Alec (*holding her*) We could collude very quietly in my room.
Dr Blackwell There's only a certain amount of my reputation I'm prepared to lose.

They kiss passionately

Paul comes quickly out of the study

Paul Hullo young lovers. . .
Alec (*jumping away from Dr Blackwell*) Jesus!
Paul No, only me.

Dr Blackwell moves away embarrassed

(*Sweetly*) Karen.
Dr Blackwell Hallo, Paul.
Paul Well, isn't this cosy.
Alec I didn't think you'd be here.
Paul Apparently. I slipped in unannounced.

Alec is curious. Dr Blackwell feels awkward and indicates going

Dr Blackwell I'd better. . .
Alec Yes.
Paul Yes.
Dr Blackwell I'm on call.
Paul Why worry. Unplug the phone. Have fun.

Alec glares at Paul and escorts Dr Blackwell to the door. They say good-night and Alec closes the door behind her

Paul pours a scotch

Alec Jealousy makes you look very shoddy.
Paul Here. (*He thrusts the scotch at Alec*) A little nightcap to drown your sorrows? I want to talk to you.
Alec More whittering? I've heard nothing but whitters from your lips since the day you were born.
Paul Now that's almost amusing. An evening at the pub has obviously stimulated your little grey cell.
Alec Good-night, Paul. (*He takes his drink and sits down with a book*)
Paul We've things to discuss, old brother, so don't appear remote. (*Paul*

waves the remote in front of Alec) And when he got there the briefcase was bare.

Alec Give that back to me.

Paul *(with sudden anger)* You could have killed her.

Alec Don't be ridiculous.

Paul My mother! Helpless on that stairlift because of this little toy. Terrified by curtains and doors with a mind of their own; and your stupid phone calls. For what, Alec? A little more power. Well if you expected her to come running and offer you the company on a plate you underestimated her. She still has more backbone than you'll ever have.

Alec I just wanted to protect her.

Paul Protect? That's a good one! Well, I've nipped your little plan in the bud. *(He pauses)* Now the usual price for silence is money. And far be it from me to break the tradition.

Alec What are you slithering towards? I shan't give you a penny.

Paul Not directly. Don't be so crude. No, my company expense account is the area I was contemplating. I want you to vote me a nice fat increase.

Alec Or?

Paul I will write everything down for mother to read. Even if you deny it the doubt will always be there. She always believed me over you.

Alec So, it's a little brotherly blackmail.

Paul Brotherly support — for which I need the envelope.

Alec Envelope?

Paul Containing the maternal goulash you and Doctor Freud cooked up.

Alec That is a genuine report.

Paul Don't stall, old brother, just hand over.

Alec reluctantly takes the envelope from his briefcase and throws it at Paul, who holds it up with the remote

Evidence; in case you forget. Now, the case for the prosecution isn't quite finished. Uncle Victor wants a turn with the cane.

Alec looks as Paul indicates the study

I think I should tell — I know who tampered with the brake fluid.

They look at each other — understanding — and Paul turns towards the study; Alec stops him

Alec Paul.

Paul comes to him

Why don't you suggest he stays the night.

Paul doesn't commit himself — instead he knocks flamboyantly on the study door

Paul Uncle Vic-tor!

Victor enters and sits confidently

Alec What a welcome committee this has turned out to be.

Victor Somewhat better than you deserve.

Paul Old Vic wants to talk to you about the Mounties.

Victor You remember the recent board meeting where you vetoed my suggestion of an office in Canada.

Alec Of course. The reason this company remains successful is because I maintain the guidelines established by my father.

Victor His guidelines are changing. You're to open our new Canadian office.

Alec Never.

Victor Diana and I have agreed.

Paul I think you'll come to like it in Moose Jaw.

Alec I wouldn't go away and leave mother in your hands. You've been trying to roast your chestnuts in front of her fire for years.

Victor What a tawdry little remark.

Paul Don't be too defensive Uncle Victor. I heard conversation in the air tonight that went waaay back.

Victor Diana and I have always been close.

Paul Marriage proposals are close.

Alec Marriage? You won't marry my mother.

Victor There won't be much you can do about it from the other side of the Atlantic.

Alec I'd never let you be part of this family.

He lunges at Victor's throat, pushing him back into the chair. Victor struggles to free Alec's grip. Paul jumps in quickly to pull his brother away, leaving Victor spluttering and holding his throat

Paul Enough, old brother. Enough.

Victor You nearly bloody choked me.

Alec Stay away from her.

Paul (*holding Alec off*) You don't need to do this alone.

Alec moves away and Paul helps Victor up

Paul Now, I'll help poor Uncle Victor up to a little cabin in Bedfordshire.

Victor is unsure but Paul appears to be on his side

(*Sotto*) It's best.

Victor acquiesces and Paul helps him to the stairs. He switches on the upstairs lights. Alec picks up his scotch

Alec Yes — make him feel at home. Why not give him some of father's things to wear?

Victor starts walking upstairs

Paul Would you like the stairlift?

Victor (*turning quickly*) No!

Paul What an athlete! (*He follows upstairs*)

Victor, still rubbing his throat, stops to look at Alec

Victor I've seen to it, Alec, you won't get away with this.

Victor exits

Paul and Alec look at each other a moment before Alec lifts his drink to his lips

Paul Why not mix that with Canada Dry? (*He continues up the stairs*) Twice in four years. What a stud! You should seek a doctor's help.

Alec reacts as Paul exits; the upstairs lights go off

Alec downs his drink, pulls off his tie and jacket and throws them into a chair. He pours another drink, looks at the portrait and sips. His head clears. He puts down the glass, goes to the desk and takes a key from a drawer

He goes to the study, switches on the light and enters

He unlocks a cupboard, returns carrying a shotgun, closes the door and turns off the light

He puts the key back and rummages through several drawers before finding cartridges in a case. He loads the gun and rests it down as he puts the cartridge box away. He removes the phone lead from the wall and lays it on the floor. He takes the red manuscript from the desk and places it on a shelf at about Diana's head height. He then adjusts the spot's beam to fall on it. Satisfied, he turns off all the other lights except the portrait, picks up the gun and his scotch, toasts the portrait and sits in the chair under the stairs. Only his arm is in view, holding out the glass. He drinks and his arm returns to view

The Lights slowly fade to Black-out

SCENE 2

As the clock strikes the first of three the Lights fade up as before

After a moment a light comes on from the bedroom area and Diana enters wearing a smart dressing gown. She notices the spotlight is on and the stairlift is at the bottom of the stairs

Diana (*to herself*) How did my chair get down there?

She leaves her stick against the banister and starts cautiously down the stairs

Alec wakes and drops the glass

　Who's that? Alec?

Clutching the banisters she moves down a few more stairs — unable to see

Alec rise from the chair under the stairs holding the gun

    Paul?

Alec Mother?

He steps out, then lays the gun in the chair

Diana Stay where you are.

Alec It's me. Alec.

Diana I know who it is.

At the bottom of the stairs she hurriedly reaches for the switch and turns the upper lights off and the main lights on

Alec Let me give you some help.

Diana I don't need your assistance.

Alec You nearly fell.

Diana Don't come any closer.

He does

    I mean it!

Alec As you wish. (*He moves away and picks up the glass*) I didn't mean to startle you.

Diana What would you expect sneaking about at three in the morning.

Alec Is that the time? I must have dozed off in the chair.

Diana Age creeping up on you? Falling asleep downstairs.

Alec It's a very companionable chair.

Diana One full of surprises. What are you doing?

Alec Nothing mysterious. I met Karen in the pub. She made me realize I had behaved rather . . . overbearingly earlier. I came back to apologise to you.

Diana How unlike you.

Alec I was also concerned about you being alone.

Diana I've come to realize I don't mind being alone. It's only the people who disturb my solitude that bother me. (*She sits at the desk*)

Paul, wearing a dark pyjama top and jeans, creeps silently onto the gallery and peers down

Alec Is it true that Victor proposed to you?

Diana How on earth. . .?

Alec Is it? (*He pauses*) It must be. You can't marry him, Mother. What about father? The family name meant everything to him.

Diana He didn't actually propose. He thought he did. But you know that as you were hiding in the study.

Alec I wasn't. That was your precious Paul.

Diana Don't you even have the guts to stand up for your own prying?

Alec Don't you have the sense to accept one home truth about him?

Diana I will when I hear one from you.

Alec I'm sure, for instance, you didn't know he is in the house.

Diana He. . .comes and goes; it's not unusual.
Alec Just unexpected. How do you think he got in? Well I'll tell you — he let himself in; without keys. I saw him — using your remote to come in at the garden doors.
Diana It doesn't matter; Paul wouldn't harm me.
Alec Neither would I. Oh what's the good — you have never accepted one single thing from me have you?
Diana I can't trust you, Alec. I know all the things you've done.
Alec I admit I have been trying to frighten you but it wasn't to hurt you.
Diana Oh, you wouldn't hurt me. Just frighten me to death. What a distinction.
Alec I was always out there. . .
Diana No doubt.
Alec . . .seeing you came to no harm.
Diana Please stop this nonsense.
Alec You see, you won't believe that, like you won't believe it was Victor who sabotaged *Night Travellers*.
Diana I've heard from Bud Mather. I understand you manipulated the promotion budget.
Alec Of course Bud will tell you that. He and Victor have pocketed most of it in a New York bank account. Victor didn't think I'd find out. He knew you wouldn't. Tomorrow I'll prove it to you. I'll also show you his business in Germany. It's banking; with an account full of lovely Chapman Deutsche Marks.

Paul creeps off but makes a noise

Alec and Diana look up

Diana More noises in the night.
Alec Not mine — this time.

Diana sees the shotgun

Diana What is the gun doing there?
Alec I loaded it for you, Mother.
Diana (*rising*) I expect you did.
Alec I'll put it away again if you prefer.
Diana No, I will.

They both move for the gun but Diana gets there first. Alec steps back and leaves Diana holding it

Alec I keep telling you, if you're worried, get rid of it. You've hung on to too many of father's things.
Diana Your advice is most generous. I must avoid giving you the pleasure of "I told you so". If you're staying you'd better go up to bed. I have work to do.

She lays the gun on the desk

Alec Why not change your routine for once?

Diana (*sitting*) With two fine sons in the house to guard me I shouldn't find it necessary.

Alec Are you planning to send me to Canada?

Diana For a while. Yes.

Alec This is Victor's idea isn't it?

Diana It won't be for long. And it's a big step up for you. We need someone reliable out there. It will give you a chance to prove yourself. I have every faith in you.

Alec Don't lie to me. You think I can't see what you're up to? Once I'm out of the way the glory path is open wide for your adoring Victor.

Diana Your father would have sent you if he'd considered it best.

Alec Whenever you used to punish me you always did it in father's name, never your own. Well this time I'll do something in his name and I'll do him proud. (*He picks up his clothes*) And another thing, Paul is aware of some intimate details of my marriage. They're not true but if he didn't make them up he must have heard them from you. It's interesting that you have so much faith in me that you would choose to belittle me in that way. Good-night, Mother.

He opens the study door and switches on the study light

Diana (*rising*) Alec. . .

Alec You want to work — work!

Diana No. . .

He exits, switching off the main lights leaving only the spot and an area of low light around her desk

Alec (*off*) Good-night, Mother.

He shuts the door and as Diana slowly returns to the desk the study light goes off

She takes the gun off the desk and props it up in the chair near the study. She pours a drink, sits and tries to work. She begins typing then looks for the red manuscript. She lifts papers on the desk and looks in a drawer before seeing it on the bookshelf. Curious, she rises and crosses slowly towards it. She tentatively reaches out both hands and picks it slowly from the shelf. As she turns away a man's bare arm reaches dramatically through the books for her scattering books to the floor. Diana screams and the hand quickly withdraws from sight. Diana grabs the shotgun and points it at the study door

Diana (*yelling*) Come out. I've been expecting you.

Paul enters quickly upstairs

Paul Mother? Are you all right?

Paul starts down the stairs as the study door slowly opens. Diana turns the anglepoise towards the study

Diana Step out where I can see your face.

She switches on the anglepoise as Alec steps forward

There is a bang and blue flash at the fuse box in the lobby and all the lights go out. Only the VDU remains on, casting a ghostly green light

Paul What the. . .? (*He comes downstairs*) Give me the gun, Mother. It could be dangerous.

Diana Don't come any closer. I'll shoot.

Paul Mother — give me the gun.

Victor appears in darkness at the top of the stairs wearing Richard's pyjamas and dressing gown

Victor Diana?

Alec (*stepping out*) Father!

Diana No!

With one quick reflex action Diana looks at the figure, raises the gun and fires. Victor yells loudly with pain and falls backwards, shot. There is a long silence before Alec turns Victor's lamp to his face and switches it on

Alec Well — that was really much more successful than I could ever have imagined. (*He is precise and in control as he relieves the uncomprehending Diana of the gun*) Paul, check the fuse box while I help mother. Anyone would think she'd been frightened by something. (*He helps her to the chair near the study*) I'm sorry, Mother, I forgot to tell you we had a house guest. He's not going to think much of your hospitality is he? Paul! The fuse box!

Paul reacts automatically

I expect it's the trip switch. The lights blew when mother switched on her lamp.

Alec switches off the anglepoise lamp as Paul goes to the fuse box and pushes up the trip switch. A few lights come on creating a dramatic effect

Alec walks confidently with the gun to look onto the landing. He turns back, smiling

Diana Alec — what have you made me do?

Alec Don't you know? (*As he talks he lays the gun on the desk and pours a large scotch*) You pushed me too far. Canada indeed. That would have been too easy? Victor would have liked that. I had to make you kill him.

Diana Victor?

Alec I had to prove to you something would work through my initiative — it has; with your help and little brother's. I worked it all out you see. I've been driving you to it. Seeing how unbalanced I could make you; and I've succeeded. You're still a great shot. Mind you, from this range you couldn't possibly miss.

Diana My poor Victor.

Alec (*moving towards the stairs*) Victor was a jealous, greedy manipulator. He stole money from the company and was going to steal you from us. Someone had to protect our interests. Ours is a family business. I wasn't going to have that man living — who killed my father.

Diana What?

Paul It's true. Victor caused the car crash. I only found out for sure tonight. (*To Alec*) But you didn't say when I got him to stay in the house it would end like this.

Alec puts his unfinished drink on the small table at the foot of the stairs and climbs the stairs confidently

Alec Don't worry, mother will get away with it. She has witnesses — we saw a lady of diminished responsibility accidentally shoot a man trying to impersonate her husband.

Diana Oh my God!

Alec Paul gave him some of father's things to wear.

Paul He wasn't supposed to die.

Alec Of course he was; wearing a dead man's pyjamas. Superstition. (*He reaches the top of the stairs and looks off. He turns back — unsure*) Paul, look in the study then go up the back stairs. He's not here but there's blood. He must be up here somewhere.

Paul Why don't you go to hell?

Alec This is why father never really liked you — because you can never see anything through.

Paul You get yourself out of this one.

Alec You're in it whether you like it or not. Now give me the gun.

Paul doesn't move

Give it to me!

Paul reacts to the anger and gets the gun. Alec comes half-way down the stairs to take it

I'll look for Victor — you phone Karen; tell her to send an ambulance. Say there's been a slight accident.

Paul (*picking up the phone*) It's dead.

Alec Here, use the one in my car.

Paul drops the phone as Alec throws him his car keys and exits R

Paul hesitates

Diana Quickly, Paul.

Paul runs off through the front door pulling it to behind him

Diana looks nervously up

Please hurry, Alec.

The study door opens slowly and Victor emerges menacingly behind her carrying an old hunting knife

His other hand is covered in blood as is the arm and shoulder of his

dressing gown. In spite of the pain this causes him he thrusts the knife at Diana's throat

Victor Don't scream.

She gasps

I said don't scream. If you scream I'll kill you now. Don't imagine I feel any compassion. After what you've done to me it'll be self-defence

Diana Victor, I swear I didn't know it was you when I fired.

Victor Who did you think it was? Richard? Not much point shooting at ghosts.

Diana I didn't know. Alec called out and I just fired. He's had me so confused — so terrified — I didn't know what I was doing. Why would I think it was you? You went hours ago.

Victor I had some unfinished business that couldn't wait till morning. Now get up.

As she stands she looks hopefully upwards

Diana Alec. . .

Victor It's no use calling for him. I left the balcony door open. He'll think I'm in the garden. (*He begins forcing her towards the stairs*)

Diana What are you going to do?

Victor Give you one last ride on your chairlift. I've made a few modifications.

Diana So it will look like another accident? I hear you're good at those.

Victor Richard's car you mean? That was a misunderstanding. I didn't mean to hurt you — then. Richard drove to the party alone. While he was inside pouring alcohol down his throat I was outside pouring fluid from his brakes. I didn't know you were coming to drive him home. By then it was too late. But I meant to kill him. He'd taken everything from me. You. The company. Everything he had was taken from me and I wanted it back. I made you an offer tonight. If you had accepted it would all have been different.

Diana No it wouldn't, Victor.

Victor No, it probably wouldn't. That's why you're going in this chair now. (*He forces her towards the stairlift*)

Diana Victor, please let me go.

Victor Not this time.

Diana For God's sake.

He turns her towards the seat as Alec runs onto the balcony and aims the gun

Alec Victor! Stop!

Victor turns in surprise to look at Alec. Diana slips from his grasp and grabs the glass of scotch from the table

Diana Victor!

As he looks she throws the scotch in his face

Victor throws his hand up to cover his face and stumbles backwards onto the stairlift. His wet hand drops against the control panel on the arm and presses a button. Blue flashes and sparks fly out all over the stairlift. Victor shakes violently for his few moments of electrocution before slumping dead. A little smoke oozes around him

Diana moves slowly away as Paul rushes in through the front door

Alec comes a little way down the stairs

Diana Alec, Paul, you were right — this is a family business.

CURTAIN

FURNITURE AND PROPERTY LIST

ACT I
SCENE 1

On stage: Wood shelving
Books
Framed photographs
Objets d'art
Hi-fi
Desk. *On it:* computer keyboard and VDU (practical), paper
    knife, telephone with amplifier, anglepoise lamp, remote
    control. *In the drawer:* key, cartridges
Desk chair
Waste-bin
Drinks cupboard. *In it:* drinks, glasses
Large portrait of a moustached man in a fedora
Coat hooks in the lobby. *Hanging on one:* a fedora
Large armchair
Three small tables. *On one:* a vase of flowers with card. *On*
    another: a table lamp
Chiming clock
Pictures
Wing chair
Electric stairlift or wheelchair

Off stage: Diana's coat and briefcase. *In it:* papers and diary (**Dr**
Blackwell)
Diana's suitcase (**Alec**)
Tray of coffee (**Alec**)

Personal: **Dr Blackwell:** bottle of pills
Diana: walking stick
Paul: bunch of flowers
Alec: watch (worn throughout)

SCENE 2

Re-set: Photographs turned inwards
Flowers
Diary on desk

Set: Vodka and tonic

Strike: Coffee tray

Off stage: Newspapers, books, manuscripts, flowers (**Victor**)

Personal: **Dr Blackwell:** Slim, black file case. *In it:* Filofax, file, pills, pen

SCENE 3

Re-set: One red-covered manuscript on the desk, two different coloured manuscripts on the table

Strike: Newspapers, glasses

Off stage: Briefcase. *In it:* remote control. Tray of food (**Alec**)
                 Ice and lemon (**Alec**)
                 Bag, large manila envelope (**Dr Blackwell**)
                 Book (**Diana**)
                 Pills (**Paul**)

Personal: **Paul:** pocket organizer

ACT II
SCENE 1

On stage: As before

Off stage: Lamp, wrapped gift (**Victor**)
                 Gun lighter (**Paul**)
                 Briefcase. *In it:* envelope containing medical report (**Alec**)
                 Shotgun (**Alec**)

Personal: **Victor:** work-glove, screwdriver

SCENE 2

On stage: As before

Off stage: Hunting knife (**Victor**)

Personal: Car keys (**Alec**)

LIGHTING PLOT

Property fittings required: patio light, upstairs light, downstairs light, outside light, study light, bedroom light, spot light, portrait light.
Practical fittings required: desk lamp, table lamp
Interior. The same throughout

ACT I, SCENE 1 Morning
To open: bright, sunny light
No cues

ACT I, SCENE 2 Dusk
To open: lamps on

Cue 1	**Diana** flicks on the patio light *Snap on patio light*	(Page 15)
Cue 2	**Diana** switches off the patio light *Snap off light*	(Page 15)
Cue 3	The door bursts open *Outside light*	(Page 15)

ACT I, SCENE 3 Early evening
To open: Upstairs light on

Cue 4	**Alec** switches on the lights *Snap on downstairs lights and lamps*	(Page 18)
Cue 5	**Diana** switches off the upstairs lights *Snap off upstairs lights*	(Page 19)
Cue 6	**Paul** switches on the upstairs lights *Snap on upstairs lights*	(Page 22)
Cue 7	**Paul** soft-shoes along the gallery and off *Snap off upstairs lights, leaving only the spill from the bedroom light*	(Page 22)
Cue 8	**Diana** switches on the study light *Snap on study light*	(Page 24)
Cue 9	**Diana** switches off the study light *Snap off study light*	(Page 24)
Cue 10	**Paul** switches off the upstairs lights *Snap off upstairs lights*	(Page 25)

Cue 11	**Diana** dims the lights using the remote control *Fade lights leaving only desk lamp, portrait light* *and table lamp*	(Page 27)
Cue 12	Table lamp crashes to the floor *Black-out*	(Page 27)
Cue 13	Music increases *Low light comes on outside*	(Page 28)
Cue 14	**Diana** screams and falls to the floor *Light outside goes out*	(Page 28)

ACT II, SCENE 1 As before
To open: darkness

Cue 15	**Victor** switches the lights on *Bring up lighting*	(Page 29)
Cue 16	**Diana** pours a drink *Lights go out one by one*	(Page 34)
Cue 17	Upstairs curtain opens a little *Glimmer of moonlight*	(Page 34)
Cue 18	**Victor** switches on the lights *Bring up lights*	(Page 34)
Cue 19	**Victor** switches on the upstairs lights *Snap on upstairs lights*	(Page 34)
Cue 20	**Victor** switches the lights off *Snap off upstairs lights*	(Page 34)
Cue 21	**Diana** turns the upstairs lights on *Snap on upstairs lights*	(Page 36)
Cue 22	**Diana** turns the downstairs lights off *Snap off downstairs lights*	(Page 36)
Cue 23	**Diana** exits *Snap off upstairs lights, then bedroom light*	(Page 36)
Cue 24	**Victor** switches the anglepoise quickly on and off *Snap anglepoise on and off*	(Page 36)

Cue 25   **Paul** switches on the lights   (Page 37)
         Snap on downstairs lights

Cue 26   **Paul** switches on upstairs lights   (Page 42)
         Snap on upstairs lights

Cue 27   **Paul** exits   (Page 43)
         Snap off upstairs lights

Cue 28   **Alec** switches on the study light   (Page 43)
         Snap on study light

Cue 29   **Alec** switches off the study light   (Page 43)
         Snap off study light

Cue 30   **Alec** switches on a small spotlight and turns off   (Page 43)
         the other lights
         Snap on spotlight, snap off the other lights

Cue 31   **Alec** drinks and his arm returns to view   (Page 43)
         Fade to black-out

ACT II, SCENE 2 The early hours
To open: Darkness

Cue 32   The clock strikes the first of three   (Page 43)
         Fade up lights as before

Cue 33   After a moment   (Page 43)
         Snap on bedroom light

Cue 34   **Diana** turns the upper lights off and the main   (Page 44)
         lights on
         Snap off bedroom light, snap on downstairs lights

Cue 35   **Alec** switches on the study light   (Page 46)
         Snap on study light

Cue 36   **Alec** switches off the main lights   (Page 46)
         Snap off main lights

Cue 37   **Diana** returns to the desk   (Page 46)
         Snap off study light

Cue 38   Bang and blue flash   (Page 47)
         Black-out

Cue 39   **Paul** pushes up the trip switch   (Page 47)
         Bring up a few lights

5

EFFECTS PLOT
ACT I

Cue 1   **Diana**: "It does that as well? Yes."   (Page 7)
A Bach concerto plays loudly

Cue 2   **Diana**: "Do them good."   (Page 7)
Cut music

Cue 3   **Paul**: "...into the home beautifully."   (Page 7)
Bring up music

Cue 4   **Paul** points the remote control at the front door   (Page 7)
Sound of bolts shooting across

Cue 5   **Alec** silences the hi-fi   (Page 7)
Cut music

Cue 6   **Alec** shoots the bolts   (Page 10)
Bolts shoot across the door

Cue 7   **Diana** shuts the door   (Page 10)
Car drives away

Cue 8   **Diana** turns thoughtfully away   (Page 10)
Bach concerto plays loudly

Cue 9   **Diana** moves to turn it off   (Page 10)
Music stops

Cue 10   To open scene 2   (Page 10)
Wind blows gently

Cue 11   **Diana** rubs her eyes   (Page 10)
The clock begins chiming five

Cue 12   **Diana** looks   (Page 10)
Telephone rings, then stops

Cue 13   Telephone stops ringing   (Page 10)
Wind rattles garden doors

Cue 14   **Diana**: "...didn't I, Richard?"   (Page 11)
Telephone rings

Cue 15	**Diana** presses a button for amplified speech *Victor's voice as script, page 11*	(Page 11)
Cue 16	**Diana**: "It's happened a couple of times." *A car is heard in the drive*	(Page 11)
Cue 17	**Diana** unlocks the door with the remote control *Sound of bolts shooting across*	(Page 11)
Cue 18	**Diana**: "Allow me to know my own son." *Wind rattles the garden doors*	(Page 13)
Cue 19	**Diana** looks out at the night *Telephone rings*	(Page 15)
Cue 20	**Diana** switches off the light *Telephone stops ringing*	(Page 15)
Cue 21	Door bursts open *Wind swirls leaves into the lobby. (Optional)*	(Page 15)
Cue 22	**Dr Blackwell**: "...and was cremated." *Telephone rings twice and then stops*	(Page 17)
Cue 23	**Dr Blackwell**: "Now please..." *Telephone rings*	(Page 18)
Cue 24	**Dr Blackwell** answers the telephone *Telephone stops ringing*	(Page 18)
Cue 25	**Paul** opens the door *Bring up wind effect*	(Page 25)
Cue 26	**Paul** closes the door *Wind effect fades but remains audible*	(Page 25)
Cue 27	**Diana** shoots home the front door bolts with the remote control *Sound of bolts shooting across*	(Page 27)
Cue 28	**Diana** switches the hi-fi on with the remote control *Hi-fi comes on low*	(Page 27)
Cue 29	**Diana** works distractedly for a while *Telephone rings*	(Page 27)
Cue 30	**Diana** switches on the amplifier *Telephone stops ringing, man's voice as script page 27*	(Page 27)

| Cue 31 | Garden doors burst open
Wind effect increases | (Page 27) |
| Cue 32 | Black-out
Music increases | (Page 27) |

ACT II

Cue 33	**Victor** closes the garden doors *Wind fades*	(Page 30)
Cue 34	**Diana** starts the stairlift *Clock strikes ten*	(Page 36)
Cue 35	To open scene 2 *Clock strikes three*	(Page 43)
Cue 36	**Diana** switches on the anglepoise *Bang and blue flash from fuse box*	(Page 47)
Cue 37	**Diana** raises the gun and fires *Gunshot*	(Page 47)
Cue 38	**Victor** presses a button *Blue flashes and sparks fly out all over the stairlift, followed by smoke*	(Page 50)

STAIRLIFT PLOT

ACT I
SCENE 1

Cue 1   **Diana:** "It isn't Concorde."   (Page 2)
         Stairlift descends

Cue 2   **Paul:** "And provides a taxi service."   (Page 7)
         Stairlift ascends

Cue 3   **Alec** stops the stairlift   (Page 7)
         Stairlift stops

Cue 4   Bach concerto stops. Brief silence   (Page 10)
         Stairlift descends

SCENE 2

Cue 5   **Diana** gets onto the stairlift and starts it moving up (Page 15)
         Stairlift ascends, then stops half-way

Cue 6   **Dr Blackwell** picks up the remote control and   (Page 15)
         presses a button
         Stairlift ascends

SCENE 3

Cue 7   **Diana** sits on the stairlift   (Page 19)
         Stairlift descends

Cue 8   **Paul** starts the stairlift   (Page 22)
         Stairlift ascends

Cue 9   **Paul** starts the stairlift with an engine noise (Page 25)
         Stairlift descends

ACT II
SCENE 1

Cue 10   **Diana** starts the stairlift   (Page 36)
         Stairlift ascends

Cue 11   **Victor** presses a button at the bottom of the stairs (Page 36)
         Stairlift descends

PRINTED IN GREAT BRITAIN
BY BLACK BEAR PRESS LTD
CAMBRIDGE